Negotiating

By Louis Zeman

Free membership into the Mastermind Self Development Group!

For a limited time, you can join the Mastermind Self Development Group for free! You will receive videos and articles from top authorities in self development as well as a special group only offers on new books and training programs. There will also be a monthly member only draw that gives you a chance to win any book from your Kindle wish list!

If you sign up through this link http://www.mastermindselfdevelopment.com/specialreport you will also get a special free report on the Wheel of Life. This report will give you a visual look at your current life and then take you through a series of exercises that will help you plan what your perfect life looks like. The workbook does not end there; we then take you through a process to help you plan how to achieve that perfect life. The process is very powerful and has the potential to change your life forever. Join the group now and start to change your life! http://www.mastermindselfdevelopment.com/specialreport

Table of Contents

Introduction

Congratulations on purchasing *Negotiating* and thank you for doing so. The following chapters will provide you with the knowledge you need to become a master negotiator, but it won't happen overnight. Your skill at negotiating is like a muscle, it needs to be exercised regularly. Use the information provided as a guideline when considering the other negotiators, you face and try out tips and tactics that will work according to what feels right.

While initially it may be easy to choose poorly, it will get easier with time. Many negotiators are adept at masking their true intentions, approach each new negotiator with an open mind and try to use each experience to the fullest. At first you will surely miss out on maximizing a few negotiations and it is best to think of those as learning experiences. The path to becoming a master negotiator is a marathon, not a sprint, take your time and you will find the results more than balance out.

Chapter 1: Common Types of Negotiations

While in a perfect world, every negotiation would have a win/win outcome and everyone would walk away happy every time, this is not a perfect world and sometimes there must be a winner as well as a loser. To ensure you are the former more often than the latter, here are the most common types of negotiations that you will likely encounter along with tips to make the best of each situation.

Win/Lose

A win/lose negotiation is the most common type of negotiation that many people will experience. Negotiating the price of car, for example, is win/lose because the car has a fixed value and the purchaser is trying to work to get that price below the set value while the seller is trying to keep the price above that point. The two goals are mutually exclusive and there will be a clear winner and loser in this negotiation.

This is what is referred to in game theory as a zero-sum game. To wit, the pie will never get any bigger or smaller, the players must play the game to determine who gets the biggest slice. When faced with a win/lose negotiation your best course of action is to try and determine the other party's options if the negotiation fails as well as their minimum requirements for satisfaction as keeping the negotiation from reaching those numbers while staying comfortably away from your own minimum numbers is the key to success.

Win/Win

In those rare circumstances where the pie can expand to the point that everyone can have an equal slice, then that is considered a win/win negotiation scenario. Typically, these only occur when both parties are joint partners in a venture as even if one partner does better to start, it is still considered win/win as both parties will ultimately make money on the venture. Salary negotiations can also be considered win/win as can intra-business sales. If the possibility of a win/win negotiation exists, then every effort must be exerted to keep the negotiations as constructive and friendly as possible.

Lose/Lose

The opposite of a win/win scenario, in a lose/lose negotiation everyone is going to get burned and your goal is emerge as lightly singed as possible. Lawsuits are typically considered lose/lose as are any type of negotiation for reparations as the injured party is rarely going to receive compensation greater to the loss and the responsible party has to pay. If you find yourself in a loose/loose negotiation it is important to avoid letting feelings come into play as much as possible. If this happens it is easy for an otherwise beneficial negotiation to turn hostile and aggressive extremely quickly. Strive to keep a collaborative tone and try and determine the other party's minimum requirements for success.

Adversarial

While depending on the circumstances, lose/lose negotiations can at least start out in a civil fashion, adversarial negotiations are always extremely competitive by their very nature. All win/lose negotiations and many lose/lose negotiations end up being categorized in this way. High stakes win/win negotiations can also turn adversarial. In the worst cases both negotiators let their feelings get in the way which can in turn mean they care more about hurting the other party then their own negotiation goals. These sorts of negotiations rarely appear without warning however which means you should have time to plan out an effective strategy for success.

Bad Faith

These types of negotiations occur when at least one party negotiates while at the same time having no intention of sticking to the negotiated agreement after the fact. What's worse, a negotiation can turn to bad faith if one party only suspects the other of wrong doing. These sorts of negotiations are commonly used to delay or deter an undesired series of events or to divert one party's attention from the heart of the issue. If you suspect that the person you are negotiating with is in fact negotiating in bad faith, then your best course of action is to include one or more penalties for failing to keep up the agreement as part of the negotiations.

Collaborative

These types of negotiations are common among business partnership negotiations and other situations that are likely to result in large gains for both parties. These types of negotiations are friendly and non-confrontational and are best handled with a mix of optimism, creativity and persuasion.

Multi-party

These types of negotiations occur between more than two parties and as a result are often quite complicated and can even take months if not years to work through fully. A good example of multi-party negotiations are treaties determining international issues between two or more nations.

Chapter 2: Basics of Negotiation

From buying a house to buying something from a street vendor, being able to negotiate properly is a skill that everyone uses to some extent from time to time. Despite this, it is a skill that few people take the time to truly master. If this sounds like you, here are a few tips to get you started in the right direction.

Two ways to view negotiation

There are two primary views on negotiation which each break the act down differently. The first consists of three primary parts, substance, behavior and process. Substance is considered the actual agenda of the negotiation, the topics that the parties involved are actually negotiating over. Behavior is considered the way the two parties interact with one another, how they communicate and what their relationship is. Finally, process is considered the approach all the parties take when negotiating as well as the greater reasons and issues behind the negotiation.

The other view of negotiation breaks the process down into four separate parts which include: tactics, tools, process and strategy. Tactics comprises all of the most detailed parts of the negotiations including prepared statements and responses to the other party's statements. Tools and process work together and jointly comprise the preparation and follow through of any set steps based on assumptions of the other party. Finally, strategy can be considered the overall goal for the negotiation including acceptable outcomes down through worse-case scenarios.

Know your stuff

Before you enter into a negotiation it is important to always research whatever topic you plan to negotiate, remember, forewarned is forearmed. Likewise, this will help you have a better idea of what you want from the negotiation as well as where to start to ensure you end up where you want to be. Remember, if you aren't clear on what you want, the person you are negotiating with won't know what to give you. Before you enter into any negotiation it is important to have three numbers in mind: your ideal outcome, the worst-case scenario you would agree to in a pinch and the number which would cause you to walk away from the deal entirely. It is important to have all three numbers in your mind at the start of the negotiation so you can gauge how it is going while it is taking place and adjust your strategy accordingly.

Embrace relationships

One key facet of any negotiation is trust, if both sides cannot trust that the other will hold up their end of the agreement then no true negotiation can begin. This is not something that appears overnight however as building a relationship takes time and effort on both sides. If you do not have a lot of time to develop a trusting relationship with the person you are negotiating with then there are a few things you can try to speed through the process.

- Look for common hobbies, interests or background details
- Mind your first impression

- Ensure any promises made can be kept
- Focus on your reliability
- Try humor, if that doesn't work, try flattery
- Avoid looking arrogant or aggressive

Know the alternatives

Before you enter into any negotiation it is important to consider the BATNA (best alternative to negotiated agreement) of all of the parties involved in the negotiation. For yourself this means considering what you will do if the negotiations fall through as well as what the other party is likely to do. Understanding the results for all-sides if the negotiations falter is key if you are to determine just how important the negotiations are to all the parties involved.

Listen

Listen more than you talk. A good negotiator doesn't need to talk incessantly to control the conversation. In fact, listening will often give you insight into what the other person is thinking, sometimes without the person even being aware of what is happening. This can also help you understand the issues the other party is facing and make it easier for the two of you to reach a consensus.

Listen can also be considered an acronym for how you should behave during a negotiation. L stands for looking and acting interested in what the other person has to say. I stands for interacting with the conversation by following up and asking questions. S stands for staying focused on your goals in the negotiation. T stands for telegraphing your understanding of the topic by citing specific facts and figures. E stands for evaluating your message to ensure you are always on point. Finally, N stands for negating your feelings, good negotiators don't let feelings enter into the equation one way or the other.

Other types of communication

When it comes to many negotiations, what isn't said is nearly as important as what is. This is because both your emotions and nonverbal cues routinely affect the other negotiating party. In this case forewarned is forearmed and you can use this information to your advantage without having to resort to any specific negotiation tactics.

Emotion

Despite the fact that their effect on negotiations have really only begun to be studied in recent years, emotions have great power to shape a negotiation for good or ill. While it is important to attempt to separate yourself from your emotions while negotiating, this is a skill that many people have not mastered which means it will inherently play a part in many decisions. Positive emotion are key to coming to reasonable compromises which can ultimately promise great gains while at the same time making it easier to measure out concessions. On the other hand, negative emotions can lead to competitive or hostile feelings and can cause a negotiation to falter all because one of the parties took something the wrong way and let the issue escalate.

Understanding the influence these emotions can have is a powerful tool when negotiating as it can afford you a small measure of control over how the other negotiating party feels. When attempting to influence the way someone you are negotiating with feels, it is important to have enough of a relationship with that person that you can predict their responses to various stimuli. To do this it is important to understand their dispositional affect so you can plan around it accordingly. Dispositional affect comes in two main varieties positive affect and negative affect with either subtly affecting how each of us responds to given situations.

Positive Affect

Those with a positive affect tend to have more confidence and tend to be happier than their counterparts. This will often manifest itself in excessive confidence prior to the start of the negotiations while also making it more likely for them to suggest cooperative strategies. This theme continues throughout the negotiation process and these people will in turn be more agreeable overall and use fewer aggressive tactics throughout the encounter. When compared with negotiators who have a negative affect, those with a positive affect are known to successfully navigate more negotiations while also being less likely to negotiate in bad faith.

This comes about as those with a positive affect tend to show a pattern of better decision making processes including understanding other perspectives, problem solving, thinking "outside the box" and a greater willingness to take risk. In addition, after the negotiation process has been completed, those with a positive aspect will tend to find themselves more satisfied overall when thinking about the outcome and about the future as it relates to that outcome. It is not all good however, as those with a positive affect are habitually unable to judge their own work in an unbiased manner, instead consistently rating themselves above their actual level of performance.

Negative Affect

A negative affect has proven time and again to negatively influence the entire negotiation process, though none so much as anger. When people negotiate angry they frequently resort to more antagonistic strategies and are much less like to cooperate even if the joint solution is relatively win/win. A negative affect will sour a relationship and easily alter a person's primary goal to one that only involves beating the other side. You can use this to your advantage however as negative affect negotiators are more prone to ignoring the other party's arguments or interests which may make it easier to sneak in an extra concession or two.

Choosing the right way to talk to someone with a negative affect can make a huge difference in the outcome. They are much more likely to make self-centered decisions without necessarily thinking through the consequences so if you phrase an offer in a way that appeals to this trait then it is more likely to be accepted. Those with a negative affect are also more likely to make mistakes in general and make suggestions that reduce joint gains.

A negative affect is not all bad however as a genuine show of emotion can be a powerful determining factor in a negotiation if it is timed properly and used sparingly. In addition, it can make for a better negotiation experience in some situations including lose/lose and adversarial negotiations.

The other party's emotions

While your own emotions inevitably play a part in your decision making process, it is important to remember that the other party's emotions will also have an effect on you as well. The other emotions at the negotiation table subtly signal to you what the other person is thinking if only you take the time to look for them. If the person seems to have a positive affect it is important to keep them that way while if they have a negative affect it is important to break their current mental cycle and replace it with something more beneficial.

Besides providing clues to their owner's mental state, the other negotiating party's emotions can also affect you physically. Some emotions such as sadness and disappointment can easily lead to an automatic compassionate response in those with a positive affect which can then in turn lead to extra concessions on behalf of the sympathizing party. The following is a list of what you can expect to happen if you display a certain emotion during a negotiation.

- *Anger:* Displaying anger is most likely to induce a desire to appease by those who are not already adversarial. Depending on the other party it will either promote a desire to dominate or yield.
- *Pride:* Displaying pride is likely to cause the other negotiating party to alter their current strategy.
- *Regret/Guilt:* Displaying either of these emotions is likely to cause the other negotiating party to view you more favorably while at the same time asking for greater concessions.
- *Anxiety:* Displaying anxiety is most likely to cause the other negotiating party to view you less favorably while at the same time expecting somewhat fewer concessions.

Communicating without speaking

It goes without saying that verbal communication is the most important element of any negotiation. What is more surmising however, is just how great of role nonverbal communication also plays in the process. When dealing with another negotiating party it is important to pay attention to how they present themselves as well as their subconscious gestures and body language. Only by taking in everything that the other party is telling you will you be able to get the most out of any negotiation.

Anchoring

A common negotiation tactic is called anchoring, according to this tactic the first party to express their position gains power in the negotiation by determining the starting parameters. The same can also be said of nonverbal cues, and body language anchoring can be extremely effective when used properly. Here are a few forms of body language anchoring you can try during your next negotiation.

- Sitting at the head of the table gives you subconscious authority of the room. Alternately, if you can't claim the seat of power, placing allies on both sides of the other negotiating party can mitigate the head of the table's control.

- Making a positive first impression can go a long way towards forming a beneficial relationship in a short period of time. As such it is always important to greet the other negotiating party with a smile and a firm handshake. Likewise, it is very important to always maintain eye contact to ensure the other negotiating parties feels as though you have nothing to hide.

Deciphering the other party's non-verbal communication

In order to be a successful negotiator you need to be able to understand the other party's nonverbal cues, the ways they interact with the things that person is saying and what it means when the two are at odds. Here are a few examples of nonverbal cues and how to interpret them.

- *Laughter:* When a person laughs at an inopportune time it tends to be either a sign of discomfort or nervousness. In response you should do you best to discover the issue behind the laugh while not specifically linking your curiosity to the laugh.
- *Negative behavior and positive speech:* If the other party seems closed off while talking, drawn in on themselves or refuses to make eye contact, there is a good chance something is bothering them regardless of how positive their words might sound.
- *Clenched fists:* This is a classic example of frustration, regardless of what the other party might be saying. Clenched fists are a sign of barely controlled frustration.

How to tell if you are winning the other party over

While a good negotiator will never tell the other party what they think of them directly, each person has a number of subconscious tells which can show how they feel about a current topic.

- If the other party is receptive to what you are saying they will tend to make eye contact and smile in your direction. Likewise, an unreceptive party may clench their jaw muscles, squint or turn their head away from you.
- Receptive parties tend to sit with their arms spread with their hands relaxed in front of them or on the table. Likewise, unreceptive parties will sit with their arms crossed or with their hands in front of their mouth. Another unreceptive sign is rubbing the back of the neck.
- Receptive parties tend to sit with their legs either spread or together and when standing they ensure they spread their weight across both feet. They also tend to face towards you. Unreceptive parties on the other hand are likely to cross their legs or stand with their weight leaning on the leg which is father away from you.
- Receptive parties tend to lean forward while sitting on the edge of their chairs and make themselves comfortable in the space. Unreceptive parties tend to sit rigidly with their backs to the chair.

Things to remember

- *Start with an honest amount.* While many people find it hard to ask for an amount they really want, this severely limits their success as they force themselves to start out at a disadvantage. The only way the person you are negotiating with will give you what you want is if you ask for it. Start by asking for what you want (or more) and you will be surprised how often the other person will give it to you.

- *Concessions should come from both sides.* Another important part of preparing for any negotiation is determining beforehand what concessions you are willing to make in order to strike a deal. While a good negotiator can always get what they want, they also know that you can't have everything which is why they prioritize aspects of the negotiation to know where to give and where to take. It is also important to know when you are conceding too much and when to concede more.
- *Strive for fairness.* While a good negotiator knows how to get the most out of every deal it is important to ensure that you aren't taking too much without giving back in return. The most productive deals are the ones where neither party feels cheated as it will make any future negotiations with that party much more agreeable.
- *Always get agreements in writing.* Regardless of the agreement struck, it is always important to follow-up the negotiations with an email confirming what was discussed. While some people might find this rude the reality is quite the opposite. Putting the agreement in writing allows both parties perfect clarity on the conversation and prevents any misunderstandings in the future.

Things to Avoid

- *Never be your own worst enemy.* If the person you are negotiating with refuses an offer you make it is important to not immediately come back at them with a lower number. This is what is known as negotiating against yourself and makes you look as though you do not have a list of firm numbers in mind. If you make an offer and it is rejected, wait for the other party to make a counter-offer. If they don't present one immediately, ask what they think would be fair.
- *Never be pressured into making a deal "right now".* If the person you are negotiating with seems extremely keen on getting things finished ASAP, there is a good chance they are trying to force something through that you may not like after closer inspection. Never be afraid to take the time you need to make a good decision.
- *Never negotiate with someone who can't make the decisions.* If the person you are negotiating with takes your offer and says they have to check with someone higher up the chain of command, offer to do that yourself. This is a common negotiating trick and one that you can easily put a stop to by simply asking to speak with the person who makes decisions.
- *Never move forward if your gut says something is wrong.* If something about the deal the other party is offering seems wrong but you can't put your finger on just what it is, hold off. It is important to trust your instincts and look for red flags.
- *Never navel-gaze.* If once a deal has been struck you realize you could have made a better deal it is important to not focus on it. Learning from your mistakes and move on, lingering on them will only cause you to question future deals as well.
- *Never get distracted by ancillary promises.* Often the other party will try and throw in something shiny in an attempt to distract you from what really matters. In general, if the

other party tells you what a good deal or great promotional item something is, the best thing to do is ignore it.

- *Never be afraid to walk away.* If a negotiation is creeping dangerously close to the number at which you walk away, walk away. Don't be afraid to signal your displeasure with the way the negotiations are heading by walking away, remember the deal is bad anyway.

Chapter 3: Effective Negotiation Strategies

Before you start trying out different negotiating strategies it is important to fist determine what type of negotiator you really are. As part of the Harvard Negotiation Project, researchers uncovered that there are three types of negotiators including soft, hard and principled. Learning about your common negotiator type will in turn help you learn what type of negotiating tactics you are likely to be the most effective with while at the same time helping you know what tactics to use to counter the other party's common negotiation strategies.

- **Soft Negotiators:** These negotiators feel that negotiation is akin to competition and just want everyone to get along. As a result, their style of negotiation is gentle, and relies heavily on persuasion and the use of positive relationships to try and get the most out of a bargain. They always try and leave a negotiation on good terms with the other party and strive to always find agreement in every situation. They see the person as part of the negotiation and avoid contests of wills, instead offering solutions and trusting others to stick to their agreements.
- **Hard Negotiators:** These negotiators have no problem using harsh, all or nothing strategies when it comes to influencing the other party. If your response to someone telling you that they don't like your offer is to tell them to take it or leave it, then you are most likely a hard negotiator. These negotiators see each negotiation as a battle and the other party as the enemy. For these negotiators there can only be one winner and they will do what is necessary to ensure that they are it. They see the negotiation as a problem to be solved and count the other negotiating party as part of that problem.
- **Principled Negotiators:** These negotiators focus on the bottom line to the exclusion of commitment to one side or another. They tend to focus on the task at hand and not factor in the personal side of an issue. A principled negotiator will consider a negotiation successful if the goal of the negotiation was met based on objective reasoning, regardless of which side ultimately benefited the most. Objective criteria include things like principles of fairness, moral or professional standards, tradition and other similar ideas.

Outside of these three common archetypes, people can further be broken down by their general disposition as it relates to negotiations. While some people will have a disposition akin to their general negotiation style, others can display differing characteristics depending on how coerced they feel by the negotiations. This is another case where relationship comes into play as it can be difficult to categorize some people without seeing them in action.

- *Accommodation:* Those who are accommodating to others ae often fond of solving other people's problems. They are frequently perceptive of emotional states and can be expected to take the relationship they have to the other negotiating party into account when it comes to determining the best course of action.
- *Avoidance:* Those who are prone to only negotiating when they feel as though they are forced to can be seen as being prone to avoiding. When they do negotiate they tend to

fair rather well as their non-confrontational outlook makes it difficult to pin any agreement down.

- *Collaborative:* Negotiators who enjoy finding joint solutions to problems and almost all principled negotiators can be said to be collaborative. Collaborative negotiators can cause problems when it comes to making unilateral decisions as asking for too much input can turn a simple problem into a complex one.
- *Compromising:* Negotiators who are fond of quickly bringing an end to all negotiations through broad concessions on both sides can be said to be compromising. While being fair is generally important to these types of negotiators, their eagerness for a quick deal can lead them to making too many concessions in short order.

Core Negotiating Tactics

While there are a wide variety of negotiation tactics that are specific to certain types of negotiations, there are a few common practices that useful in almost any situation. While some of these may seem difficult at first, with some practice you will be surprised at how effective they can be.

Brinksmanship

This tactic can be risky unless you know the other party's BANTA and know that they have little choice but to reach some type of agreement. When attempting this tactic, it is important to push a middling agenda that leans in your favor so brusquely that the other party can only walk away or accept. When done properly it convinces the other party to think in a linear fashion about the proposed terms. The most effective counter to a brinksmanship tactic is to simply walk away, regardless of your BANTA, this will show the other party that they must restrain themselves if you are to move forward with any negotiations.

The bad cop and the good cop

This negotiation tactic is taken from the interrogation method of the same name; the only difference is that as long as you have convinced the other negotiating party that you can't make decision on your own you can pull this off all by yourself. To do so you simply start by listing off a number of extremely stringent specifications before apologizing for them, blaming them on someone the other party will never meet, and offering your ideal terms in a new context which makes them seem much more reasonable. Being aware of this tactic makes it easy to spot, though if the bad cop isn't present it can be difficult to verify.

Never commit first

Undervaluing their own position is a common mistake that many people make when entering into a negotiation. While purging yourself of this urge is crucial to your long term success at negotiating, it is also important to remember that the other party in the negotiation is likely struggling with the same issue. As such, if you can get the other party to put forth the first offer you will generally find yourself in the stronger of the two positions.

In addition to the fact that their first offer will frequently be better than what you yourself would have put forth, it also provides you with a general outline of their position while giving them nothing to work with in return. As such, it is then much easier to counter with a number that still meets your needs while at the same time allowing you to set the bracket for further bargaining firmly in the territory you prefer. Ensuring the other party goes first can sometimes be worth millions, just ask Brian Epstein, the Beatle's Manager. In 1963 the band's star was on the rise and United Artists Studio was anxious to cash in on burgeoning Beatlemania.

However, at the same time the studio was unsure if the band was going to go on to be the most famous band of all time or fizzle out before the film came out so they decided to put the movie out for as cheaply as possible. This meant that the band would not be receiving much of a money up front but the studio planned to offer the band as much as 25 percent of the profits from the film so if they stayed popular everyone would win. Armed with these numbers the producer headed off to negotiate with Epstein but he was smart enough to first offer $25,000 and then ask the Beatle's manager what the band wanted without first laying his cards on the table. As such, when Epstein started with an offer of 7.5 percent of the film's profits, United Artist was able to make a killing on *A Hard Day's Night* released in 1964.

Bogey
If during a negotiation the other party suddenly begins to make a large fuss over what by your estimation seems to be a relatively minor point; then there is a good chance they are deploying a bogey tactic in an attempt to trade that small point for a meaningful concession later on. If you believe you are the victim of a bogey, try and bring in a bogey of your own and note the results.

Highball/lowball
Similar to brinksmanship, negotiators fond of this tactic tend to start with either an extremely low or extremely high offer with the goal of making their second offer seem much more reasonable by comparison. It will also allow for additional concessions made on the part of the other party. This can be countered with a layered tactic, sending the unreasonable offer away makes it seem as though it is out of your hands while at the same time not allowing them to use it as an advantage later because you aren't the one who denied them.

Play the fool
Good negotiators have learned that the less the other party thinks you know the more you can get out of them. In fact, as long as you don't lose credibility doing so, there is no end to the positive correlation between apparent relative stupidity and negotiation dominance. The cause of this is two-fold, first the other party will underestimate you and as a result lower their guard; second, it is human nature to help those who are mentally below average rather than using them for selfish ends. While this isn't true of everyone, of course, it is true of enough people to make it a statistically relevant way to diffuse those who seem overly competitive during a negotiation.

To understand why this works so well consider this, think of how difficult it would be to retain a competitive edge when the person you are negotiating with is asking your opinion on the best way to negotiate with you. How would you carry out a plan against someone who responds to specific questions, not with facts and figures you can debate but rather with a simple shrug, a self-deprecating laugh and a return question "what do you think".

Likewise, if you present yourself as a competent and prepared negotiator then you almost guarantee that the other party will work their hardest to counter you. Make things easier on yourself by ensuring you never appear to be any of the following, except of course when it would hurt your credibility to the point of turning the negotiations against you (like during a salary negotiation).

- The sort of person who always knows what they want without taking the time to debate internally and think things over.
- The sort of person who can unilaterally make decisions without "running it by" anyone else.
- The sort of person who is an expert in whatever field the negotiation relates to
- The sort of person who would never concede a major point
- The sort of person whose decision is always final
- The sort of person who never needs to make notes

Playing the part of the fool allows you to retain a wide variety options which will help you maintain the advantage during negotiations. These include being able to believably request additional time to check your notes, consider or research an offer, run the decision by a board or committee or consult legal counsel. You will also be able to more easily plead for more concessions or put other pressure on the other party while still maintaining a positive relationship.

For example, if a hard negotiator comes at you saying that the deal you have proffered has a number of ambiguities, you can throw them off guard by pretending to mull over the word before sheepishly explaining that you know it sounds familiar but it's just not clicking and asking them to explain it to you. This will force them to abruptly change thoughts and possibly gloss over their issue when it comes back around. Even if they don't drop the issue completely, they will then be more likely to approach the topic without their previous vigor. Likewise, it can be used to reinvestigate a portion of the negotiation that you aren't comfortable with while not seeming aggressive yourself. Claiming you don't "quite get" something is much nicer than claiming that you think the other party is wrong and needs to reinvestigate their point.

This tactic is perhaps most effective during win/win negotiations though it will work anytime you feel the need to prevent someone from being overly competitive. Remember, never play dumb in an area that will hurt your credibility with the current negotiations but otherwise don't be afraid to try it out.

Chicken

If you find yourself suddenly blindsided by a number of unreasonable demands in response to a relatively safe offer, then there is a good chance the other party is deploying a tactic commonly known as chicken. Again, this is a tactic that can be negated by knowing the BANTA but otherwise it can be difficult to know if the other party is bluffing. When trying to bluff the other party it is important to either be able to go through with your extreme measures of have a way of backing out of them gracefully in mind before you start.

Snow job

If you feel as though the other party is constantly throwing new numbers and statistics at you then you might be a victim of the snow job tactic. If you find yourself having a hard time telling which facts are relevant, cry off and take the time you need to ensure you make the best decision. If they follow up with an artificial deadline claim the need for expert council.

Think of it as haggling

One common type of negotiation tactic that you will frequently come up against is what many people consider to be "hard-bargaining". These people will approach every negotiation from as firm of a stance in their favor as possible under the assumption that the total amount of the negotiation is fixed so they need to take as large of a share as possible. They will them use any means necessary to ensure they concede as few points as possible throughout the negotiations. The easiest way to counter these types of people is by building a relationship or if that seems to be an untenable solution then adopting your own firm stance and throwing their tactics back at them. While this is a less than optimal solution it is the only way to counter their otherwise immoveable stance. Once they start to give in a little, respond in kind, this may allow for a more beneficial dialogue moving forward.

Layer-up

As previously discussed it is important to never be seen as a person who can make unilateral positions as you can then use each additional person you can imagine a need to gather input from as a reason for a concession or set of concessions. Insulating these layers from one another is crucial as it removes the power to compromise from your purview and can allow you to trade several concessions for the promise that the rest of the negotiated agreement will be accepted.

Nibble

A nibble can be considered any seemingly small concession right before the deal is closed despite the fact that the topic was not raised beforehand. This can be a great way to get a few extra concessions from the other negotiating party though it is easily countered with a firm application of the layering tactic.

Break amounts down to the ridiculous

When a salesperson takes the cost of an item and amortizes it to the point that they can say something like, "for just 50 cents a day" that is considered breaking an item's cost down to the ridiculous. During negotiations it can be beneficial to break costs for the other party down to the ridiculous to make them seem minor enough to not bother over. Likewise, it is important to understand the full cost of any item the other party feels the need to break down in this way as it should be a red flag that they are trying to get away with something. Thus it is important to try and couch your funny money estimates in ways that will not attract notice while being ever-vigilant against those who would do the same to you. Here are a few tricks to keep an eye out for:

- Interest rate which are written as anything other than a concrete figure in currency
- Lots of talk about the monthly cost of a thing without reference to a total amount
- Cost broken down by item or by foot without mention of a total amount
- Increase broken down as hourly instead of as a total amount

Casinos know that forcing people to trade in their real money for chips makes it easier for them to spend more without thinking about the consequences and breaking costs down to the ridiculous works on the same part of the mind. Keep this in mind when negotiating and remember to always discuss costs to the other party in ridiculous terms while at the same time always considering the real world cost of your end of the bargain.

Focus on Deadlines

If you find yourself in a situation where you ultimately have the power in a negotiation, then it can be beneficial for you to set a deadline either to receive an offer or respond to an offer. Setting a deadline is a great response to a negotiator who always seems to need more time or to run the proposal through some new layer of management. It is best to have a favorable BANTA when attempting this tactic however as it can backfire if you overestimate your position.

Place your focus where it will do the most good

Good negotiators know enough to not let the way that the other party acts distract them from their primary goal for the negotiation whatever it may be. Regardless of how the other person acts it is important to always try and separate the negotiation itself from both you and the other party. While it is important to not damage relationships whenever possible, it is equally important to not let the other party's actions influence your perception of the results. Remember, there are plenty of negotiation tactics that involve using the fact that you look angry to your advantage. Never outright dismiss any idea or tactic that will not completely bring the negotiations to a halt.

The flipside of this is that is perfectly acceptable to sometimes appear upset during negotiations as long as the actuality finds you completely in control of the situation. If you let your emotions get the better of you, a safe bet is that is exactly what the other party wanted which means you have already lost the negotiation. If you find yourself having trouble keeping your cool remember to focus on the issues. Instead of letting the other party provoke you take the time to look back through the current negotiations and see how far you have already come.

React Visibly

Taking the time to inhale sharply or make a believable shocked face when being confronted with an offer you don't like can often make the other party question the validity of their offer. This is much more effective than simply verbally indicating your shock or your displeasure. Making this reaction seem natural is key however as a subconscious reaction can be seen as a signal to lower their expectations.

Auction

If you find yourself in a multi-party negotiation with more than one other party biding for the goods or services you provide you can easily use this to your advantage and play the other parties off of one another. If the other parties sense that they might be about to lose out on something this will make them want it even more, increasing your position even further.

Always part amiably

At the end of any negotiation, regardless of whether you win or lose it is always important to offer congratulations to the other party. If you have won the negotiations then this will help to make the other party feel as though they got a better deal compared to what they actually agreed to. If you have lost the negotiation however this will help maintain your relationship with the other party while at the same time planting a seed of doubt that maybe they did not win out as much as it first appears. Even if you do not feel the need to congratulate the other party it is important to never end a negotiation by gloating. You never know when you might have to negotiate with that person again and there is no reason for gloating which is worth having to face an uphill battle in a later negotiation.

Chapter 4: Tips for Negotiating a Job Offer

Regardless if you are interviewing for a position with a new company or a new position in your current company you only have one opportunity to help decide on your starting salary. The following tips will help you come out the other side with most money possible.

Think before you speak
The only time to discuss salary specifics with your employer (or potential employer) is when they have already made you an offer. Despite this fact, a common negotiation tactic for employers is to ask about salary amounts before any offer has been made as if it is just casual conversation. While decades of schooling have trained most people to answer questions correctly and truthfully when asked, in this case nothing could be more incorrect. This can backfire in two common ways, first you ask for too much money and you lose out on the opportunity by making a bad guess; second, you accidentally lowball yourself and leave money the employer was planning on giving you in their pocket instead.

To avoid this trap, ensure you never say anything concrete in regards to salary until you know that you are at least on the shortlist to get the job. If the topic comes up beforehand deflect it by saying you aren't quite sure what all the job entails yet and you don't want to speak out of turn. This can then be followed up by asking specific questions about the job to direct the conversation away from the hot button issue. If instead the other party asks about your current salary then you can disclose it, but remember, when it comes to actual salary negotiations you can talk about what the fair market value for someone with your skills in your region.

Never agree to the first offer
With few exceptions, salary negotiations will never start out at the most the employer is willing to spend. Keep this in mind and never immediately agree to the first offer that is placed on the table. This first rebuttable should be subtle however, start by starring at the suggest amount as if you are really considering it. You don't even need to say anything, instead make a noise in your throat as if you are thinking hard about it. Let this go on for 30 seconds or so and you will frequently hear a better offer soon after.

An important part of this tactic is knowing how much you are actually worth. As discussed above, it is helpful to know what someone with your skillset is worth right now in your area. Use this number to measure when your thoughtful considerations can start to actually become thoughtful. The closer to your current value the number is the less likely pretending to consider it will work. It is also important to use this trick sparingly as it loses effectiveness with each repetition.

Always consider the perks

Before you head into any job offer negotiation it is important to be well-versed in the benefits and perks that the company offers. Depending on how you use them what may seem like a small concession to the employer can add up significantly in your favor over time. Do your homework and it may pay off in the long run. Likewise, if you believe that you are brining something special to the table (and have reasonable data to back it up) it can be worth asking for new benefits as well. As long as you do not go overboard the worse thing the other party can do is say no.

Chapter 5: Tips for Negotiating Sales

When in the business of selling things, it is important to remember to always try and sell the customer first, and negotiate only if it is the only way to keep them from walking away. Not only will this tend to make you more money, it allows you to begin the negotiation knowing more about the customer, thus making the negotiations more effective for everyone.

Know your limits

While you are in the final moments of closing a sale giving the other party an extra 10 percent off might not seem like much of a concession...until you think about it later and realize how much than 10 percent eats into your commission. Having a firm idea of just how much you can do to appease the other party, before you enter into the negotiations, is crucial to long term success.

Never start the negotiations

You have already presented the other party with your best sales offer, if they want to negotiate more then let them set the terms. Doing otherwise is akin to negotiating against yourself. Always listen before you speak.

Don't estimate

While offering a range of estimates can give you some wiggle room, never offer a top of the range greater than you are willing to provide. If you quote a price reduction at 10 or 12 percent the other party is only going to hear 12 percent.

Never start in the middle

If the other party starts a negotiation by asking for half-off, a novice salesperson might return with an offer of 25 percent off and be happy they split the difference. In reality however, studies show that very few people ever expect that much of a discount. Instead of countering in the middle it is important to stay within sight of your original offer. This will imply that you are already near the lowest possible price and that the margin for variance is relatively small.

Only negotiate once

If the other party you are dealing with asks to negotiate the final price, before you do so it is important to ensure that they have the authority to close the deal without having to run any decisions up the chain of command. This is crucial for your bottom line as if you end up having to negotiate with a second party they will often want to start at the point you reached with the first party and work from there. Likewise, it is important to always way until the end of the negotiations to put anything in writing, doing so sooner will only lead to headaches later.

Chapter 6: Tips for Negotiating When Not Face to Face

Despite what many people think, negotiating with someone when you are not in the same room with them has different rules you should follow in order to ensure the negotiation ends in your favor. First and foremost, however, you should keep in mind the fact that the person who initiates contact starts from a higher perceived level of power because they are forcing the other person to put what they are doing aside and focus on the negotiation, right now. Use this to your advantage and always initiate contact whenever possible. With that in mind, consider the following additional tips the next time you find yourself negotiating over the phone or via email.

Another interesting fact which bears consideration when there are multiple negotiation avenues available is the fact that studies show that face to face negotiations tend to favor the negotiating party with the most real world power. The results are reversed in virtual negotiation scenarios, however, as when people are no longer face to face their subconscious responses to authority figures do not activate, allowing them to negotiate with a clearer mind, and leading to better results 100 percent of the time. What's more, this effect can be seen regardless of the number of people who are involved or what the specifics of the negotiations may entail.

This interesting fact of human biology can be used to your advantage in any type of negotiation scenario. It is important to keep it in mind and to use either face to face or video conferencing negotiation avenues when you are negotiating from a position of power and avoid them whenever possible if you are instead negotiating from a weaker position. Remember this fact and use it when strategizing and you will find you always have the proper mindset for the negotiation at hand.

Phone negotiations
Have a plan of action
When preparing to make a phone call that is likely to result in negotiations, it is important to never pick up the phone until you have a clear plan in your mind as to how you want the conversation to go. Only planning as far ahead as the small talk will open you up to potential conversation derailment or other distractions to creep in and prevent you from reaching your goal. Plan out your primary goals for the conversation as well as the talking points you will need to cover to attain each. While you don't need to go to the trouble of writing out everything you will say during the conversation, you will be surprised at just how effective seeing the outline in front of you during the conversation will be.

If the phone call you are making is part of a series, make sure to start each call with a recap of where things ended in the previous call using as positive a spin of the preceding events as possible. Likewise, at the end of each call, make sure you recap what ground has been covered during the call that is concluding and outline what you would like to discuss the next time a phone call is initiated. It is important to always discuss what is coming up next as nothing will damper future phone call based negotiations more than a sense that despite multiple discussions, the topic in question is essentially treading water.

Don't be afraid to do research, either prior to the first conversation or between negotiation sessions, forewarned is forearmed and having access to a wide variety real world scenarios that relate to the negotiation topics will only help your case. What's more, showing that you are extremely well-versed on the topic in question is likely to impress the other negotiator. While this will be unlikely change their position all on its own, the knowledge that you understand all sides of the issue will prevent the other person from try to blindside you with questionable facts and make the negotiation as a whole more effective.

Ensure you remain active during the conversation
When you first make contact with the other party, it is important not to jump right to business and take the time to engage in appropriate small talk. Your ultimate goal is to be as engaging as personal as possible, remember, the only connection the other person has to you is your voice. This means you are missing out on important body language opportunities that need to be filled in somewhere, take cues from the other person as far as appropriate small talk and take pains to remain as affable as possible, even going so far as to make jokes when appropriate. This will be the only chance you have to build a rapport with the other person, don't squander it.

Without physically occupying the same space as the person you are negotiating with; It can be difficult to indicate that you are engaged in what the other person is saying if you do not take the time to take notes and ask questions appropriately. You need to ensure that the other party remains as interested in the conversation as possible in order to achieve the desired results and to make it easier to win them over to your way of thinking.

Taking notes will also make it easier to make sure you are aware the instant that miscommunications arise. By not being in the same room with the other party you are missing out on potential body language cues that can clear up a variety of miscommunications on the spot; double check any potential blind spots as quickly as possible to ensure that everyone remains on the same page. Nothing will derail a potentially positive negotiation faster than a small miscommunication left unchecked until it escalates exponentially, do yourself a favor and make sure everything is as clearly spelled out as possible.

This means it is also important to give the call you are making your upmost attention. Turn off any other screens you may be looking at and focus completely on engaging in the conversation and taking notes as appropriate. Multitasking is a myth, the only thing you are doing when multitasking is working on two tasks in disjointed chunks. What's more, if you are fully engaged in the negotiations and the other person is multitasking you'll have an even greater chance of walking away with a more favorable outcome. Every negotiation is important, make the extra effort to treat them as such.

Always Follow Up

When you are in a face to face negotiation you are virtually guaranteed to have the other party's complete attention. When it comes to phone negotiations, however, the time between the point your conversation ends and the time the other person acts on the information you gave them could be substantial. This is why it is important to follow up phone negotiations with an email that verifies the details so that everyone remains on the same page. This will allow you to follow up with potential future clients in a way that will be easy to refer to in the future and to ensure that they retain your contact information while at the same time not containing the same stigma that calling to reconfirm details holds. It also allows you to remain in the other party's consciousness for a prolonged period, allowing them the extra time they may need to come around to your way of thinking.

Email Negotiations

The limitations of email when it comes to negotiations are similar in magnitude to the differences in face-to-face interactions versus those made using a telephone. When talking to the other party during a negotiation you lose out on the ability to use body language, when emailing in regards to a negotiation, you lose out on the ability to judge the other party's tone as well. This can make it difficult to judge the efficacy of attempted negotiation techniques but it also means that a simple, quality argument that is well-stated can be more effective in this medium than in any of the others. Words have the potential to be extremely powerful as they operate in more of a vacuum than other negotiation avenues, don't take this effect lightly.

Take the time to layer in some extra personality into your responses as a way to humanize yourself without going overboard when it comes to sharing personal details. Consider the following examples:

- Show that you are a real person with a life outside of the negotiation by starting you email by apologizing for the delay in your reply because you were out of the office for a medical issue, spending time with family, or something similar. Talk about how happy you are to be back at work now that things are returning to normal, though you are really swamped because of it.

- Express concern for the other party's wellbeing because of something recent that occurred such as when they took over their current position of when the person you worked with previously left the company. Express empathy, explain that you don't want to add more work to the pile, then couch the issue that needs negotiating in the most reasonable terms possible.

- Take the time to genuinely express some emotion that is typically lacking in buttoned up corporate emails. Explain how the lack of forward progress that is currently taking place has you frustrated at your own inability to push through it before connecting your feelings to those it is likely for the other party to express as well. Use the mutual feelings as a bridge to make positive inroads on the topic that you want to see resolved.

- Take the time to prepare beforehand so you can include as many questions and requests for data as possible. Giving the other party a concrete path forward will allow them to commit to the project more fully sooner than might otherwise be the case and thus be more committed overall when it comes to finding a solution no matter what. In these situations, it is important to ensure that you express your desire and confidence that a mutually beneficial solution can be reached.

When in doubt use video conferencing

While the tips above will allow you to make the most of what are otherwise less than ideal negotiation situations, the best way to ensure that you have as many of the advantages of seeing the other person as possible, is to see as much of the person as possible. These days, the high-quality internet connections and vast array of devices which also contain front and rear facing cameras means that it is easier than ever before to simply set up a video chat and see the other party's face at the very least.

Video conferencing offers a number of advantages over email negotiations, including real time reactions from the other party, but is also superior to a simple phone call as the additional information conveyed by facial expressions cannot be understated. Consider the following tips when it comes to making the most of video negotiation opportunities.

Ensure the process is as simple as possible
Just as with phone calls or emails, it is important that you initiate video conference contact with the other negotiating party to ensure you enter the negotiation from a position of power. Unlike with the other methods of communications, it is important to ensure that the video conferencing solution you use is as simple for the other person to access as possible. Selecting a confusing or finicky video conferencing solution could needlessly delay the negotiation and force the other person to start from a flustered or annoyed state which will make them inherently less receptive to whatever ideas you are presenting. Before selecting a video conferencing provider, do your homework and choose the one that is right for you.

In addition to choosing a simple to use solution for the video conferencing, it is important to email the other party prior to the scheduled meeting time to ensure they have the ability to participate in video conferencing and that their webcam is fully functioning. This will allow both parties to double check that all equipment is working properly and fix any kinks without delaying the negation itself. If the other party does not have a webcam, consider your strengths and weaknesses when it comes to negotiating and then compare the cost of a webcam to the benefits of having the negotiation go your way. Depending on the results, buying the other party a surprisingly cheap webcam may be a viable option.

Take advantage of the format
Once you have taken the time to ensure that everything is set up to allow for a video negotiation, the biggest mistake you can make is to then treat it the way you would a regular phone call based negotiation. Take the time to make the most of your ability to send and receive facial cues, project your authority when it comes to the matter in question and use hand gestures to convey your over-the-top energy levels. In addition, many video conferencing

solutions offer the ability to including multimedia portions such as PowerPoint presentations which can make up for the defect when it is compared to face to face negotiations.

Finally, video negotiations tend to end with more successful results because once you have come to an agreement most video conferencing solutions provide you with the opportunity to send over contract agreements instantaneously so that the other party doesn't have the time to rethink any of the excellent points you made while waiting for an actual contract to appear. Everyone knows that the more excited the other party is, the more likely they are going to stop thinking and start acting, take advantage of this fact and use it to your advantage whenever possible.

Chapter 7: Tips for Getting the Price You Deserve for Your Goods or Services

Be confident

When it comes to sealing the deal, many of those who work in sales remain too eager when it comes time to negotiate the final price. This comes about due to the largely mistaken assumption that if they are not willing to lower their prices they will ultimately miss out on the sale. In fact, the opposite tends to be true and clients respect a salesperson who is able to articulate why their product or service is worth paying a little bit more to obtain. Never worry about being rejected outright for the price you present, very few customers will walk away outright without discussing the specifics. Approaching this discussion in the proper way will allow both parties to walk away happy, but only if you are willing to put in the necessary work.

Next you will need to remind yourself that your price is reasonable and that you deserve to receive it; while this may sound like something that does not bear repeating, in reality it is important to repeat this affirmation like a mantra during the negotiation as it will help you to find the mindset required to make the most of the situation. When it comes to defining reasonable, remember that anything you can convince the customer to pay is a reasonable amount. Don't make the mistake of undervaluing your service, you never know what a customer is willing to pay until you ask them. The more valuable your service is, the wider the range of viable variables will be. Focus on improving overall value and let the reasonable price take care of itself.

Having confidence in your product or service is a crucial step towards getting the price you deserve for your goods or service. Since you won't be dropping your price, you instead need to be able to explain to the customer why the product or service that you are offering is worth what you are trying to sell it for, and having a persuasive, truthful reason as to why that is the case will make the entire process go much more smoothly. Don't hamstring yourself when it comes to pricing, don't just tell customers that your product or service is worth the full price you are suggesting, believe it.

When you present the price you are hoping to get for your goods or service never indicate regret over what you have presented by saying that you are sorry or that you wish there was more you could do regarding the price. This ties back into having confidence, you have no reason to feel sorry about what you are offering, because you know it is not just an acceptable price but actually a great deal at the price you offered. Getting the customer to accept your proffered price is all about framing, you only have so much time to spend with each person, make it count.

Finally, make a habit of always having several potential sales on deck at all times. If you become too committed to any one sale, slashing prices to make it a reality begins to look more and more appealing. Doing so will cause you to present yourself in an uncertain fashion when it comes time to negotiate which will then make it easier for the customer to sense your nervousness. Presenting yourself with confidence has already been discussed, knowing you have other sales on the backburner will make doing so even easier.

Prove the worth of your product or service
After you have firmly outlined the lowest price you are willing to accept when it comes to selling your goods or service the next step will be to present the information that indicates why your goods or service is worth the price you quoted the customer. The first step is to couch your price in legitimacy and the best way to do so is to compare it to the market average, if your price is above the average, determine what extra services or benefits come with your goods or service and determine what those extras would cost when paid for individually. If you cannot ultimately justify your predetermined price, then it might be time to reassess. It is important to use readily available data when making these determinations so that if the customer goes and does their own research they will come up with numbers comparable to those you presented.

You should make a point of never starting a conversation with a customer without a firm price you want to receive for your goods or service in mind. Once you do so, you will them be able to feel out the customers you speak with to assure that everyone is on the same page. If you get the feeling that you and the customer are not on the same page, there is no shame in asking them for the budget they are working with or possibly an acceptable range of prices they are interested in. This will save everyone time in the long run and help to find them a solution that works for them.

Have predefined concessions
Obviously there will always be scenarios where it makes more sense for you to play ball with certain customers, but you should always do so in a way that allows you to save face. For example, if while talking to the customer they indicate that they might have additional business in the future then it would be worthwhile to suggest a reduced rate for multiple sales up front. Regardless of the specifics, it is important that you never offer up a concession that causes the balance of power in the negotiation to slip out of your favor. Don't be afraid to offer an ultimatum, if your goods or service is worth it, the customer will always come around to your way of thinking sooner or later.

While having predefined concessions will help you stick to favorable exchanges on the fly, it is also important to make sure that you never appear too anxious to make these sorts of deals. If you offer up concessions, even those that require bulk purchases, too quickly it will make it seem as though you value your goods or service less than you actually do, a move that will cause the customer to reflect this nonproductive viewpoint. Remember, it is always best to hold out on making concessions as long as possible to artificially enhance their value to the maximum amount possible.

The ultimate goal of providing concessions is to make each customer feel as though they are a unique asset to your business that is appreciated as such. Ultimately, a satisfied customer who pays less today is always worth more than a dissatisfied customer that paid full price. To leave each customer feeling as satisfied as possible it is important to always listen to any complaints they might have. Even if you don't make any changes, as remaining firm is important, they will ultimately appreciate the opportunity you gave them to vent. Make sure you can explain the reasons behind your pricing in detail so you can answer any questions they might have before reiterating the unique strengths of your goods or service and sticking to your guns.

Be ready for common customer responses
While no two customers are truly alike, most people tend to approach negotiations using one of three main tactics. Some people like to response in an initially overly negative way either by raising their voices, choking, or making exaggerated facial or hand movements. The reality is that they are actually not all that surprised by your offer, they are simply looking to see what your response will be. If this happens to you, it is important to stay the course and wait for them to add something productive to the conversation. If they don't say anything more, your best bet is to repeat your offer and reiterate its unique value once again.

An additional tactic that is used quite frequently is when the customer counters your offer with the declaration that they can get the same product or service elsewhere for a cheaper price. The best response to this tactic is also to reiterate what about your goods or service that makes the price not only reasonable, but a bargain. During this part of the negotiation it is important to take the customer's focus off of the price of the product or service and onto how much they actually want what it is that you specifically are selling. Once you can convince them that the price is simply a small speed bump in the process, they will be more willing to defer to what you have already established.

Another common tactic that many people, especially those who appear weak, frail or as though they are already dealing with tragedy often attempt is explain their situation in the most tragic way possible before explaining that they only have X amount to spend on your goods or service and that's that. When confronted with this scenario it is important to remain completely nonplused by what you are hearing, reminding yourself that it could just as easily be a lie as the truth if required.

Showing any response to the information that they present will open you up for further attempts along these lines and will make it much more difficult to have a conversation that is productive to either party. Instead of giving in, call their bluff by asking about their finances and appearing as though you are considering what they tell you and how they can draw from other areas to afford your product. Reemphasizing the value of what you are offering is also a valid strategy.

You are halfway done!

Congratulations on making it to the halfway point of the journey. Many try and give up long before even getting to this point, so you are to be congratulated on this. You have shown that you are serious about getting better every day. I am also serious about improving my life, and helping others get better along the way. To do this I need your feedback. Click on the link below and take a moment to let me know how this book has helped you. If you feel there is something missing or something you would like to see differently, I would love to know about it. I want to ensure that as you and I improve, this book continues to improve as well. Thank you for taking the time to ensure that we are all getting the most from each other.

Chapter 8: Tips for Negotiating with Creditors

While many people think of debt as a fixed amount which is set in stone, the reality is quite the opposite. In fact, many creditors will settle for between 25 and 50 percent of the total amount owed which means it is in your favor to attempt to negotiate over debt whenever possible. With that in mind, it is important to do some homework before attempting to negotiate with creditors.

First and foremost, it is important to understand that negotiating with creditors can take several attempts but nearly all types of unsecured debt can be settled for no more than 50 percent of the original total. If you cannot reach this sort of agreement the first time, do not be afraid to walk away. On the flipside however, understand that the creditor will continue to call, send letters, even threaten legal action until the negotiations are completed. Throughout this process it is important to know how your creditor is likely to act next and to understand if your debt is secured or unsecured.

While it is easier to avoid paying the full sum on unsecured debt, it is important to remember that there are laws in place to limit what attempts to collect on a debt can entail and even how long a debt can be attempted to be collected upon. It is also important to consider the legal costs of bringing a suit against you versus the amount of money you owe. Legal battles are expensive and it will rarely be in their best interests to follow through on a court case, regardless of their threats.

The following suggestions work with any type of creditor or local debtor though the success rate can vary depending on the type of debt owed. Local business people, unsecured loans, credit card companies and loans made from local banks are often easy to modify. Meanwhile, student loans and any loan that came from a major bank is much more difficult to negotiate better terms for.

Always start with bankruptcy
Regardless of how likely a scenario bankruptcy is for you, explaining to the creditor that you have been having a hard time making payments and have been looking into every available option can make them much more receptive to negotiating. As a rule, creditors will get less from a person who has declared bankruptcy, even if they have a legitimate claim to the debt which means their negotiators are told to do whatever is possible to ensure that doesn't happen.

Be ready to make a payment
For creditors, getting some money now is better than nothing indefinitely. This is why it is a good idea to explain that you have the cash on hand now to pay off a percentage of the debt (under 25 percent) and start the negotiations there. Make sure you explain that you have a certain amount of the debt on-hand (and make sure you do) and are ready to make a settlement payment immediately or within a few days.

Chapter 9: Tips for Negotiating Large Purchases

When it comes to negotiating for large purchases such as vehicles there are a number of standard tactics which apply in the search for the best deal.

Regardless of what you are told the price is always negotiable
Most sales people will be looking to break the price of the item down to the ridiculous and will be interested in talking about the monthly payment versus the total cost. Start by asking to negotiate with the person who will have the final say and don't let them discuss anything but the total price of the vehicle, after taxes and fees.

Set fixed terms for the negotiation
Start by determining what amount you are willing to pay for the item by researching average prices in your area. Insist on a price as near your goal as possible and stick with it until the other party gives in. Assuming you did your research and your offer is reasonable there is no reason they should not be able to work with you on reaching an acceptable price and until they do don't let them move the conversation to another topic. If they instead ask about trade-ins, explain you are looking into your options but don't want to discuss it until the price has been finalized. If they instead ask about extras, pass.

Regardless of whether it is true or not, when asked about financing say that you are already approved for a loan and are willing to pay with cash, though you would be interested in hearing about dealer-financing. Only allow this topic of conversation once the final price has been negotiated. If the other party continues to try and negotiate the price, again refer to your starting offer and explain that you are not interested in wasting anyone's time with excessive price negotiations and that you are prepared to leave rather than going back and forth indefinitely. Any further conversation along these lines should be met with a stony silence. If you get transferred to a more senior sales associate it is important to repeat the previous steps verbatim and to continue this process until then know you are serious. Following this pattern will guarantee you are in control of the situation.

Initially the other party will most likely issue a blanket denial, claiming that the dealership will not allow the vehicle to go for such a price. At this point it is helpful to have research you can point to and explain that other dealerships seem willing to meet your demands. If the other party continues to use a layer tactic, ask to speak with someone who has more authority.

Keep your loan short
If you must take out a loan to afford the purchase it is important to keep the terms as short as possible. Vehicles and similar items depreciate every year which means the longer you are paying for the vehicle the less of a return you are getting on your money.

Chapter 10: Tips for Negotiating Prices When Buying a Car

As previously discussed, in face to face negotiations the person with the most power starts at a natural advantage. While the person who is selling a car, especially at a dealership, is generally that powerful person, there are a number of tactics you can employee in order to even the odds, or even, turn them in your favor. When you first begin the search for a new vehicle it is important to visit numerous dealerships while looking at what is available while always keeping a few things in mind to make any potential future negotiations more likely to go in your favor.

When looking at available stock, it is important to let the salesperson know that you are just browsing at the moment and have no intention of buying today. This will frame all future actions in a positive light while also keeping the sales person from pressuring you too thoroughly. Feel free to give out general descriptions of the cars you are interested in but avoid specifics that include price ceilings or questions about trade-in value or monthly payments as those are likely to come up much later in the process. Getting ahead of yourself at this point could lock you into an unfavorable starting negotiation position. Whatever you do, be polite and courteous to the salesperson as you will likely be dealing with them if you do plan on using that particular dealership to find your new car.

Know the right time to submit your ultimatum
First and foremost, you should start every car buying experience by presenting the salesperson with a well-researched and reasonable offer and telling them that they can contact you when they are able to meet it. While this won't always result in immediate success, it will likely work in your favor sooner than later. It is generally a good idea to present your offer to a salesperson around the middle of the month and then follow up two weeks later when the end of the month rolls around. Enough time will have passed to show that you were serious about walking away while also allowing you to check on the vehicle you were interested in without losing face.

Your reappearance at the end of the month also provides them with the opportunity to get one more sale in, a real boon especially if the rest of the month happens to be subpar when compared to their average. This also goes for coming back at the end of the night on a Saturday or days that were terrible for people window shopping thanks to inclement weather or important local events. Getting the best deal from a dealership is simply a matter of picking the best moment that tilts the balance of power in your favor.

Dealing with a private seller
When it comes to buying a vehicle from a private seller there are a few important things that should be assessed in order to determine how much variance you can expect to get out of the price. Many private sellers have external reasons for selling the vehicle that may make them more open negotiation, when finding out additional information about the vehicle it is important to always ask to why the other party is selling the vehicle and see if the story behind it can be used to your advantage. Using the information that you have acquired, you can then make an opening offer on the vehicle that is somewhat lower than the listed price but make up

the additional value by pointing out the fact that you can get the full offered amount in cash that same day. The promise of an easy end to their time with the vehicle is frequently enough to push most people over the edge towards a sale.

Don't be afraid to ask questions
Regardless of who you are buying the vehicle from, you should never be afraid or nervous to ask the seller how flexible they are on the listed price. While on the surface this question doesn't seem very useful, after all, practically everyone selling a vehicle is open to negotiation, at least to a partial degree. In reality, however, the answer to this question and the way it is answered can provide you plenty of valuable negotiation information. In general, the more enthusiastic their response, the more flexible the price is. In addition, they could give out useful information including the floor on the price or additional tidbits that could come in handy later.

If the information you are given in return doesn't make it sound as though you and the seller are going to realistically be able to make a deal, it is important to never give up hope before making a thorough effort to make the most of your situation. Even if your budget is below the stated minimums it will never hurt to explain your maximum and see what happens in response. As long as you do so politely and explain that what you are saying is in an effort to save everyone some time, you will be surprised at how many additional doors it may open. Always tell the seller to give you a call if anything changes; you never know what will happen if you are willing to wait long enough.

Don't get anxious
If a negotiation starts to swing in your direction, especially if things happen much more quickly or more easily than you initially imagined, it can be perfectly natural to get excited and work to close the deal right there on the spot. However, it is important to never get so caught up in the excitement of winning a negotiation that you forget to have any type of used car inspected thoroughly prior to signing any documents. An ounce of prevention is worth a pound of cure, if the vehicle is in good condition then the seller should have no problem waiting for you to have it completely checked out before making a deal.

Negotiate Separately
After the salesperson has agreed to your offer, it is important to remember that if you are not paying cash for the vehicle, you will want to negotiate the amount you are getting for your trade-in (if any) as well as the terms of repayment separately. This will allow you to negotiate each part of the scenario individually so you don't lose out in one area to benefit in the other.

When it comes to negotiating what your trade-in vehicle is worth, it is important to do research beforehand to ensure you know what you are working with. Likewise, if you have made any improvements to the vehicle it is important to be able to point them out and to have a reasonable idea as to what additional value they bring to the vehicle. When it comes to negotiating the terms of your repayment, it is important to remember that lower isn't always better as the interest rate tends to spike with each additional 12 months added to the repayment plan which means the overall amount you will be paying for the vehicle increases significantly. Remember to stay within your means when it comes to picking a new car and avoid the potential headaches of trying to find ways to pay for it later.

Chapter 11: Tips for Negotiating Prices When Buying/Selling a House

There are few things more stressful in life than either buying or selling a home. While the housing market is nowhere near as tumultuous as it once was, that hasn't made the experience easier for anyone involved. Here are a few tactics that you can use no matter what side of the process you are on:

- Remain silent, this is good advice regardless of how you are submitting offers or counter offers. The response to an offer sets the tone for the remainder of the negotiations and if you take the time to simply act self-assured at your price while appearing completely comfortable with the silence then the other party has no choice but to respond. To seal the deal, repeat your current offer after 30 seconds of silence have passed, don't elaborate just repeat the facts. The likely response to this tactic is a concession from the other side, make it count.

- Take advantage of body language, when you are in the same room as the other party, take advantage of that fact by using body language to convey negative emotions without appearing needlessly argumentative. A well placed wince can set the stage for the type of negotiations you want moving forward while forcing the other person to acquiesce to you before the real negotiations have even started.

Regardless of which side of the experience you are on, however, there are negotiation tactics that you can use to ensure that you come out the victor once the dust has settled.

Getting the best deal when buying a home
When it comes to buying a new house, the most important thing to remember is that in order to make a realistic and competitive offer on a particular home you need to be familiar with the local market, including specifics as close to your desired lot as possible. Outside of what other properties in the area have sold for, it is important to understand what the supply versus demand is like in the area in question. For all of these reasons, it is often best to hire a realtor who can help you to more easily understand the unique facts about your potential new home. Beyond that, it is important to enter into any negotiations preapproved for a mortgage so you can have the confidence to negotiate specifics knowing you can follow through. Keep the following in mind once you have found your dream home and are looking to close a deal.

Be flexible
While everyone likes to win when coming out of a negotiation, when it comes to buying a home, it is important to focus on any serious issues that may need addressing instead of squabbling over amounts under $10,000. For example, the difference between a home that is $200,000 and $205,000 is only $21 per month. Take the concessions the other party asks of you seriously and determine their true costs before committing either way. It is important to remember what is truly at stake for these negotiations and not to let the perfect home slip away in an effort to win an ultimately minor point.

Regardless of whether or not the area you are looking in can be considered a "buyer's market," it is important to ask for concessions, including repairs, on the part of the seller. There is no harm in asking as long as you are not overly committed to the changes you requested. It is generally best to wait until you have had the property inspected to make these sorts of requests as you will not have the chance to make them again once the terms have already been made. Prior to entering into negotiations it is important to also determine why the seller is moving and what, if any, concessions that this information may contain. If you know the seller is looking to modify the closing period or has other personal needs that relate to the home, you can better use these to bargain for concessions of your own. Go into the negotiation phase prepared for anything and you'll walk away happier, guaranteed.

Placing the right offer
When it comes time to formally submit an offer, it is important to base it on what the actual value of the home is worth, rather than on the list price. Take into account where the price is in relation to homes in the area and pick your battles, the price for homes listed below market value is unlikely to budge, while those that are listed above value are worth the effort of true negotiation.

Especially when it comes to competitive markets, it is important to ensure your offer is appropriate for the property in question as taking chances on a lowball offer can easily result in that offer being ignored as the seller moves to the next one on the list. Be competitive, not insulting. If you really like a property, there is no shame in asking for an inspection prior to the point where negotiations begin, remember you only get one chance at negotiation, make it count.

Let the negotiation begin
Once you are ready to negotiate on the price of a home, you will need to determine a negotiation strategy based on the information that your research revealed about the area in question. If the area you are looking to purchase property in is a buyer's market, you as the buyer, unsurprisingly, have the power going into the negotiation. This means that properties are likely to take much longer than normal to sell which in turn means that sellers are anxious to do as much as they can to keep potential buyers interested.

The best way to take advantage of this situation is to start by making as many demands as possible in order to concede some of them in exchange for the ones you want the most. A few popular choices include:

- Start with an offer that is approximately 10 percent lower than the amount you ultimately wish to pay for the property.
- Ensure that the seller will pay all of the closing costs on your time table.
- Ask for appliances or large pieces of furniture, lawn furniture etc.

If the market happens to be in the seller's favor, then buyers have much less clout and the wrong type of offer can cause you to lose out on the home you had your eye on. In these scenarios, a reasonable, firm offer that is quickly made tends to be the best course of action. When it comes to contract contingencies, you will only be able to negotiate for things like inspection and appraisal, otherwise the seller holds all of the cards.

If the market that you find yourself in has an appropriate number of houses for sale, then it is important to go into any negotiation expecting it to take longer than in either of the more extreme scenarios as personal priorities on either side are likely to expose themselves leading to multiple counter offers. In these situations, it is important to know what concessions are crucial for the other party to make and what concessions you yourself will never be comfortable making. Your initial offer in this scenario should be below the asking price and include reasonable contingencies as well as a few that swing for the fences to give yourself some room to come to an agreement. More so than other scenarios, neither party is likely to proceed if they don't feel as though they are profiting from the negotiation.

Getting the best deal when selling your home
When it comes to selling your home, you are likely to hear all sorts of crazy offers and plenty of crazy buyers making unreasonable demands for concessions. In addition, it is important to take the time early on to divorce your feelings for the home from the selling process as otherwise it can be difficult to let negative comments slide which can lead to counterproductive exchanges between buyers and sellers. That's why it is important to keep the following tips in mind in order to ensure you walk away from your former home as well off as possible.

Selling can give you leverage in bank mortgage negotiations
If you are behind on your mortgage, the fact that you are now selling your home can give you a significant edge in negotiating with the bank on your past due bills. In these scenarios it is important to seek out the head of the loss mitigation department of your lender and bluntly explain the specifics of your situation. As long as you explain the entirety of the scenario, you will be surprised how willing most lenders are to wait for, or to otherwise reduce, payments. A foreclosed property helps no one, working out a solution in these situations is in everyone's best interest.

Remain vague
Prior to any eventual negotiations, you will want to remain as tight lipped as possible when it comes to explaining to any real estate agents or potential buyers the reasons you decided to move. Events such as moving for a new job, getting a divorce or having difficulty paying the mortgage are all things that can be held over your head in hopes of getting a better price on the property because it is clear that you are in a hurry to sell. Instead, it is important to already have a simple, easy answer when someone inevitably asks you why it is you are selling your home. Blame it on the weather, your spouse's family, or even the strength of the current housing market, whatever your excuse is, stick to it and keep it vague.

Counter aggressively
Assuming you are not in a seller's market, the first offer that you receive from potential buyers will likely be a lowball bid designed to get you to come down from your asking price to start the

negotiation off in their favor. The way that most sellers counter this offer is by coming back with something lower than their list price but higher than the price the buyer offered. This will certainly help move the process of selling the home along, but it will also go a long way towards dropping the total price you can expect to see for the home.

Assuming you took the time to research the current fair market price of your home, countering with your list price shows that you know what you have and that you stand by your initial assessment. While some buyers will ultimately walk away when confronted with this approach, many more will come back with a more reasonable offer that you can then work with more readily. If you don't want to appear inflexible while at the same time retaining as much of the list price as possible, instead concede a nominal amount, something like a thousand dollars, to show that you are not completely inflexible.

Reject the offer flat out

Depending on the offer the buyer submitted, a simple counteroffer at your listing price may not be enough, if this is the case, the right course of action may then be to simply reject their offer outright and invite them to submit something more suitable instead. This sort of response is only really viable when you are certain that your listing price is fair for the quality of the property in question. If the buyer returns with a second offer, even if it is just a few thousand dollars higher, you will enter into the negotiation proper from a greater position of power.

This strategy also keeps you free to play the field in hopes that a more appropriate offer comes along while the initial buyer is deciding whether or not to submit a new offer. The fact that this is the case will also motivate the original potential buyer, assuming they are still interested, they will then want to move quickly to lock down the property or risk losing out completely. This is particularly the case if the property has been listed recently or if a public showing is pending.

Create an arbitrary timeframe

Another way to create a more powerful negotiation position for yourself is to place the house on the market but refuse any offers prior to a date that is typically after an open house. This will plant the idea in potential buyers' minds that there is already competition for the property, even if there really is none. This strategy almost always results in higher initial bids and may even lead to a bidding war if there are multiple interested parties.

The same goes for any counteroffers that you submit once an offer on the property has been made. These are legally binding negotiations and it is important to treat them as such which means it may be in your best interest to put a timeframe on your offer to ensure that you are not put in a position where a better offer comes along that you are unable to consider because you are already in negotiations with a buyer who is taking their sweet time coming back with a counter to the counter offer. The key is setting a deadline that is pressing while at the same time not so short that the buyers don't have time to return another offer. Consider a timeframe that is one day less than the standard limit for such things in your state to show buyers your serious about moving forward with the home selling process.

Make the right concessions

When it comes to negotiating with buyers, agreeing on who is going to be paying the closing costs can be a real sticking point in otherwise productive meetings. These fees can often be difficult for buyers, already strapped for cash from the process of buying and moving into a new home, to attain in a reasonable period of time and can easily result in otherwise qualified buyers having to move on to a new property, leaving your home stuck on the market.

In these scenarios it is important to remember that the buyers are already borrowing a substantial sum so adding a comparable amount to the cost of the home can be a reasonable concession on both ends to make the sale a reality. However, it is important to remember that the total cost of the home must be reasonable based on the appraisal, otherwise the lender on the loan might not approve it.

Understand what draws buyers to houses

For most buyers, buying a new home isn't about getting the greatest possible value for their money, it is about making a real connection with a house as a place that could be home. As such, when you are selling, it is important to hold off on lists of facts and figures regarding amounts spent remodeling and maintaining and more about making the extra effort to show your home in the best light possible. Letting people talk themselves into making an offer without getting into the nitty gritty will keep you from appearing needy or over eager which will allow you to negotiate from a place of power instead.

Be aware of common tactics

There are a number of common types of negotiation tactics that buyers will try that can all be mitigated with the right response. The first common type of buyer is the sort who is always going to have to run any numbers past a third party before giving any type of concrete answer. It is important to not be fooled, however, as this is simply a way to try and cut down the final price a little more. Stop this strategy in its tracks by asking buyers if there is anyone they would like to be present in order to finalize the specifics. A similar tactic is the good cop/bad cop routine where the one party is extremely enthusiastic while the other is extremely negative. The solution here is the same, negotiate with all parties at once.

Another common buyer negotiation tactic is to try and get you to agree to a number of small concessions that ultimately add up to a surprising amount. To counter this strategy, take the time to precisely document everything that has been agreed to on both sides and refer to the document when additions are suggested. Remind them that an agreement is already in place and that changing anything now would result in a new offer having to be submitted. A variation on this technique is the buyer who instead blurts out an offer, usually quiet favorable to them, in an effort to shock you into agreeing.

Finally, buyers may ask what are known as trial balloon questions, which are questions that are designed to feel out the seller while not revealing any new information about the buyer. Trial balloon questions include things like how firm the list price is, or if you would be interested in financing the property without a lender. If you find yourself constantly bombarded with questions, retaliate with some of your own by asking what their response to your response might be.

Chapter 12: Negotiation Tips for Introverts

Negotiating for anything, much less important things like salaries and the price on major purchases likes cars and homes can be difficult for anyone, but for those with introvert personalities it can seem practically impossible. The first step to making the negotiation process possible, if not pleasurable, is to understand that there are plenty of people in the same boat and to know that this particular issue can be overcome with practice. The secret to being able to successfully negotiate as an introvert is to stop trying to act like an extrovert and to instead play to the strengths that being an introvert offers.

Have a clear goal

Make sure you take the time to visualize a clear goal before you start any negotiation. If you head into things by simply hoping for the best, it is likely that your natural tendencies will take over and things will go down a less productive path. Prior to entering into the negotiation it is important to research the topic thoroughly and understand your personal reasonable limits in advanced. Having a clear understanding of what lines can and cannot be crossed beforehand will make any actual negotiating much more manageable.

If it seems as though the person you are negotiating with is either unwilling or unable to help you reach your reasonable, and in all likelihood attainable goals, you must be willing to walk away. This isn't a rude behavior or one that will have negative consequences later on, no matter what your brain might tell you to the contrary, this is simply a thing that people do when negotiations don't go as planned. Stick to your guns and you will see positive results.

It helps to understand that you have value

When it comes to any negotiation, but especially those that involved trained sales people, the entire negotiation process can be made to seem much more manageable as long as you keep in mind the fact that the person you are dealing with ultimately wants your business. Negotiation doesn't have to be about conflict, in many situations you can still save yourself a substantial amount of money without sacrificing the other party's happiness. Don't let your imagine get carried away, the only thing that will happen if you try and fail to manage a successful negotiation is that the price of the goods or service in question will remain the same, there is no real downside when it comes to negotiating.

Use silence to your advantage

As an introvert it is likely that you are used to silence more than the average extrovert and negotiations are one of the rare times that you can use this fact to your advantage. When the person you are negotiating with says something that you don't agree with, silence is one of the most poignant ways to make this fact known. Don't be afraid to let the silence linger, state your piece and let them fill in the blanks with nervous chatter, doing so will leave you in a position of power for whatever comes next.

Know yourself

If you are like most introverts than being out amongst the populace is a draining experience from which you need to recharge in order to remain at your best. If this is true for you, then do yourself a favor and schedule negotiation sessions first thing in the morning so you are at your best when it comes to interacting with others. If this is not an option consider email negotiation, or possibly even something over the phone, to prevent the pitfalls of personal interaction. You will be surprised at just how much of a difference the right mindset will make when it comes to negotiating successfully.

The same is true when it comes to focusing on the task at hand. Don't worry about the other party, focus on your goals for the current negotiation and don't let interpersonal factors cloud your judgment. As long as you did the required research on the topic in question then your request is most likely perfectly reasonable which means you have every right to voice it with certainty. With that in mind, all you need to do is to choose a role that can best get you the things you are looking for. The person you are negotiating with doesn't know the real you which can provide you with the opportunity to act the way a person would who is looking to get the most out of the current scenario. Give yourself the freedom to try out different roles and you will be surprised at the results.

Take the right tone
Negotiation can be difficult for introverts because it can be difficult to determine the right level of friendliness as compared to aggressiveness. In most scenarios the best choice is to go with a mix of friendly yet forceful, aim for the tone that actors use in movies where they call someone friend, except it is clear that the two people are decidedly not friends. You want to make it clear that you are being reasonable while at the same time projecting the fact that you will not be pushed around.

If you find that type of tone difficult, consider the benefactors of the results, are you working to get a better price on a new car to ensure your kids can get to where they need to be on time? What about the future spouse and child that will share the new home with you if you can only afford it? Maybe you simply want a bigger yard for your dog to call home. Regardless, think about who you are really negotiating for and you will be surprised how much easier it is to take what is rightfully yours.

Practice, practice, practice
If you remain nervous about an upcoming attempt at negotiation, consider practicing with a friend or loved one beforehand to mitigate performance anxiety. Practicing vocalizing the things you want can go a long way towards making them easier to say when the time is right. This exercise can also help you to understand the back and forth flow that is part of many negotiations, practice until you are comfortable taking the time to think offers through rather than agreeing out of reflex. Take the time you need to make the decision that is best for you and don't forget to get everything that has been said in writing, just in case.

Chapter 13: Surprising Goods and Services You Can Negotiate For

While everyone knows to expect to haggle when it comes to common things like raises and buying a car, the best negotiators understand that when it comes to trying to get a better deal, nothing is off limits.

Cell phone and Internet contracts

Contrary to what the companies providing you with these services want you to believe, the amounts that you pay for them are actually quite flexible. If you take the time to call them up and make it seem as though you are interested in cancelling your service; you will be surprised at how willing the person on the other end of the phone is to suddenly make a deal. If the first person on the phone insists that there is nothing they can do, ask for the customer retention department. The company is interested in keeping you as a customer as opposed to trying to find someone off the street to replace you, make them work for it.

Furniture

When it comes to large items like mattresses and couches, the manufactures of these items tend to set a minimum that they can be sold at which companies can then adhere to or possibly mark them up from there. Stores that sell them at the existing prices will tell you so and those that don't will instead be willing to work with you in some capacity, either way, you win. Even if the price is non-negotiable, consider asking for additional benefits or items with your purchase, at the very least you should be able to get them to throw in free shipping even if it is not typically offered.

When it comes to finding places willing to negotiate, always look for family run stores as opposed to chains and don't underestimate the allure of paying in cash. In these scenarios it is important to always ask to speak with the owner directly. When doing so, keep in mind that furniture is often marked up as much as 75 percent over purchase price, remain firm and don't be afraid to leave your number and walk away. While it isn't a quick or easy way to purchase new furniture, it will work at least as often as not.

Medical Expenses

When it comes to medical expenses that are not covered by your insurance, hospitals and doctors' offices typically have systems in place to ensure they at least are able to get paid for some of what was originally owed. Medical expenses are the most commonly unpaid form of debt so many institutions are willing to work with you rather than take a potential loss. This doesn't mean they will do so willing, however, and you will need to persevere through what is likely going to be several layers of red tape before you reach someone who will make a concession. Remain firm in your assertions that you cannot in anyway pay the amount present and you will eventually begin to make headway.

Vacation days

When it comes to getting the most out of a new job, most people take the number of vacation days they are presented with for granted. However, in scenarios where the monetary budget is tight, asking for a few extra paid vacation days to balance things out is a surprisingly painless for everyone to get what they want out of the negotiation. To make the most out of this negotiation tactic it is important to research trends in similar jobs in your industry, once you find a few examples of perks outside of what you are being offered, consider how they compare to your complete package and if your new job comes up wanting consider how best to compare the two and make suggestions in regards to corrections.

Gym memberships

Gym memberships are another scenario where the prices are actually quite a bit more flexible than they initially might appear. For example, those who sign up or renew their memberships around the beginning of the year are likely to get better deals, the same goes for the end of the summer when gym memberships typically drop off as the desire to look good by the pool wears off for another year. If you aren't interested in waiting, instead consider doing research as to average membership prices and after getting a free trial membership, bring your findings to the person who is in charge of customer retention. Remain firm in your commitment to a better deal and you will be surprised what you can get away with.

Professional services

There is no law setting the cost for the services provided by professionals like lawyers and dentists. This means that there is nothing to stop them from offering you a better deal if you are simply willing to ask for it. Any time you are quoted a price, there is no reason not to try and make it a little bit more reasonable. Keep in mind that the worst thing that anyone is ever going to say is no and you will be surprised how malleable even the most set in stone prices really are.

Conclusion

Thank you again for choosing this book. Hopefully it has been able to provide you will all of the information you need to take your negotiation game to the next level. Remember, negotiation is a skill and like any other skill it requires practice to master properly. Find the time to practice negotiating minor matters with friends and strangers and use the time to learn to read body language and anticipate arguments on the fly. Over time you will find that complex tactics come to you unbidden when the need for them arises; and even better, you will have created a number of your own.

If you found this book useful in anyway and feel the need to leave a star rating or review, thank you, it is most appreciated.

Free membership into the Mastermind Self Development Group!

For a limited time, you can join the Mastermind Self Development Group for free! You will receive videos and articles from top authorities in self development as well as a special group only offers on new books and training programs. There will also be a monthly member only draw that gives you a chance to win any book from your Kindle wish list!

If you sign up through this link http://www.mastermindselfdevelopment.com/specialreport you will also get a special free report on the Wheel of Life. This report will give you a visual look at your current life and then take you through a series of exercises that will help you plan what your perfect life looks like. The workbook does not end there; we then take you through a process to help you plan how to achieve that perfect life. The process is very powerful and has the potential to change your life forever. Join the group now and start to change your life! http://www.mastermindselfdevelopment.com/specialreport

Beginners Guide to
Investing

Free membership into the Mastermind Self Development Group!

For a limited time, you can join the Mastermind Self Development Group for free! You will receive videos and articles from top authorities in self development as well as a special group only offers on new books and training programs. There will also be a monthly member only draw that gives you a chance to win any book from your Kindle wish list!

If you sign up through this link http://www.mastermindselfdevelopment.com/specialreport you will also get a special free report on the Wheel of Life. This report will give you a visual look at your current life and then take you through a series of exercises that will help you plan what your perfect life looks like. The workbook does not end there; we then take you through a process to help you plan how to achieve that perfect life. The process is very powerful and has the potential to change your life forever. Join the group now and start to change your life! http://www.mastermindselfdevelopment.com/specialreport

Introduction

Introduction

Money is an extremely important part of our lives. We need money to buy things, pay for services and also reserve some for the future. However, the salary we earn ends up being too less, owing to growing inflation and increasing needs.

So what can we do to increase our monthly income and have enough money for the future? Well, investing your money is a good choice it will help your money's worth increase over time.

There are several investment options to choose from but none of them prove to be as enticing and lucrative as stock market investments.

Stock market investments refer to investing your money in buying financial securities that are traded in the share exchange market. These investments are easy to make and you can easily increase your monthly income.

But in order to invest, you must have enough knowledge about these markets and know exactly how to invest in them. There are many small, and big, details to consider before you start investing your money in the stock market.

In this book, we will look at the stock market in detail and understand everything that there is to, about stocks, bonds, etfs and precious metals. We will also look at some tips for you to manage your money and trade wisely.

I hope this book helps you in making the right financial choices for yourself.

I want to thank you for choosing this book and hope you enjoy it.

Chapter 1: Stock Market Basics

The stock market is a big market place, where financial securities are traded on a daily basis. People, worldwide, buy and sell these securities every day, in order to earn an income from them. If you have watched the movie, "The wolf of wall street", you will have a fair idea of how the stock market operates.

In this chapter, we will look at some of the basic concepts that relate to the stock market.

What is it?

The stock market is a physical market where companies list their stocks. These companies can be big or small and will float their shares in the market. These shares are bought and sold on a daily basis. Apart from company shares, other financial securities such as bonds, etfs, commodities and precious metals are also traded in the share market. There is a separate market for each and you can trade in all of them or some of them depending on your needs.

There are two types of markets namely the physical market and the virtual market. The physical market is where brokers trade in stocks on the floor of the market. The most famous physical market in the world is the New York Stock Exchange or NYSE. Here, many multi national companies from all over the world list their stocks for people to buy and sell. If you wish to trade here then you have to be a member of the stock exchange.

The other type of stock market is known as the virtual market. These virtual markets are online markets and you can trade in them by creating an account. There are no brokers here and you can buy and sell by interacting with other members of the stock market. The most famous online stock market is NASDAQ.

You can choose to trade in any of these markets or both.

Basic components

There are many components in the stock market but only a few of them are basic namely the stock markets, the brokerage firms, the brokers and the demat account. Let us look at each one in detail.

Stock market

As you know, the stock market is a place where you buy and sell financial instruments. It is a market place where buyers and sellers meet to satisfy their investment needs. It can be a physical or a virtual market. You can trade in any one of them or both. There are many stock markets all over the world and that are all inter linked owing to sharing common stocks.

Brokerage firms

As was mentioned earlier, you need to be a member of the stock market if you wish to buy and sell shares. But it is not easy to become a member and you have to pay a lot of money to do so. So instead, you can sign up with a brokerage firm and trade in the market. There are many firms to choose from and you must look for the best one that is well reputed.

Brokers

Brokers are employed with brokerage firms and will help you buy and sell shares. They will charge a commission for their services. There are two types of brokers, one being full time brokers and the other being part time brokers. Full time brokers will dedicatedly work for you and invest your money. Part time brokers will only buy and sell your stocks and will not assist you in the decision making process. You must pick a broker based on your requirements.

Demat account

The demat account is what you will need to trade with in the stock market. This account is not like you regular bank account. There was a time when it took people several days to buy and sell stocks. But now, it takes only a few seconds to do so. This is only possible if you have a demat account.

Basic terminologies

Here are some basic terms that you must get acquainted with to start trading in the stock market.

Stocks: Stocks are shares of companies that are sold in the stock market. These shares will help a person own a part of the company. Stocks are the most preferred stock market investment choices.

Bonds: Bonds are financial instruments that are either listed by companies or the government. Bonds are issued to the customer at a value that is much lower than its face value.

Etfs: ETFs stand for exchange transfer funds. ETFs are like mutual funds but traded in the stock market. They are like regular stocks but with the benefits of a mutual fund.

Precious metals: Precious metals are also traded in the stock market these include gold, silver, platinum etc. These are traded on a daily basis just like stocks.

Commodities: commodities are every goods and items that are traded in the stock market. There are many categories of commodities like livestock and energy that are all traded in the stock market.

Foreign exchange: foreign exchange refers to foreign currency that is traded in the stock market. These are foreign currencies that are traded on a daily basis.

Basic techniques of trade

Intra day trading

Intraday trading refers to trading in the stock market on a daily basis. You can buy and sell stocks daily. This is an advanced form of trading and you must take it up only after studying the stock market for some time. The risk and reward are both quite high in this form of trading and you can undertake it to earn a daily income.

Short term trading

Short term trading, as the name suggests, refers to trading for a period less than 6 months. So you buy and hold a financial instrument for less than 6 months and then dispose it off. Short term trading is a lot like intra day trading as the time period varies between a week and 6 months.

Long term trading

Long term trading refers to holding a stock for a long time. This time will vary from instrument to instrument. This is said to be a safe option and will give you consistent returns provided you invest in the best stocks and other instruments.

Chapter 2: FAQs On The Topic

It is obvious that you will have a few doubts, when you take up a new topic. In this chapter, we will look at the various FAQs on the subject and understand the topic of stock markets better.

What is trading in the stock market?

Stock market trading refers to buying and selling stocks. These stocks are valued at a certain price and the basic intent is to capitalize on its revised price. So you must buy a stock at a low price and then sell it at a higher value. There are many categories of stocks to choose from including IT, pharma, construction etc. You must sign up with a brokerage firm and then start trading in shares. Apart from these shares, there are many other financial instruments that are traded in the market. We will look at each one in detail in the chapters to come.

Who is it for?

Stock market investments are for everybody, interested in increasing their capital's worth. The market does not discriminate and anybody can partake in the buying and selling. As long as you have the capital for it and are willing to take a risk, you can take part in the stock market. Right from working professionals to students to housewives, the stock market welcomes everybody with open arms. But before you decide to invest in it, you must understand everything that there is to and only then start trading in stocks and other financial securities. That you can do by going through this book and reading on the stock market essentials.

Is it a safe choice?

No investment is a safe choice and everything comes with a certain amount of risk attached with it. If you think it is a safe bet for you to invest in the stock market then you are wrong. There are many things that can go wrong and you must be prepared for them. If you tread cautiously then you will not experience any problems. But that does not mean they are not present. It is of utmost importance that you understand carefully all the different concepts and only then can you decide to jump into the stock market. So basically, there are no guarantees in the market but you can minimize the risk by making smart choices for yourself.

Can I become rich overnight?

This is a big misconception that many people have when it comes to stock market investments. They assume that they can capitalize on a few good stocks and double or triple their money. But as I said, it's a misconception and the stock market will not make anyone rich over night. Patience is extremely important and you will have to wait it out before realizing any substantial profits. If you are in a hurry to see results then you will end up settling for a loss. So don't have unreasonable expectations from the stock market.

Is it a full time job?

Not necessarily. If you employ a broker then he or she will buy and sell your stocks so that you can only pick the stocks and the time to buy and sell. But if you wish to do intraday trading then you might have to take it up full time as the prices of stocks change every second and you have to make quick decisions. If you think your stock market trade is going very well then you can consider taking it up full time and making it your day job.

Can I buy and sell by myself?

Yes. Although you need to sign up with a brokerage firm, you can buy and sell stocks by yourself. You need not always rely on your broker to buy and sell your stocks. You might end up wasting time in doing so. You will be given access to your demat account and you can start trading by yourself. It might take you some time to understand how it works but once you get down to doing it, it will start getting relatively easier for you.

Will I be charged for it?

Yes. You will be charged a minimum commission by the brokering firm, as you will be using their services. So even if you refuse to take the help of the broker, you will still have to pay a fee for it. But that is only fair given you are using the firm's membership in the stock market to buy and sell your stocks. If they weren't present then you wouldn't have the chance to buy and sell stocks. The choice is fully yours. You can choose to employ the services of the broker or buy and sell the stocks by yourself.

How long will results take?

Results will not take long to show provided you do all the right things. Patience is vital and you will have to study the markets for some time before investing in the stock market. If you try to hurry things up then you will have to settle for a compromise. Understand that it is your hard earned money being invested in the market and you must do all the right things for it. Don't have unreasonable expectations from it as the higher the expectation, the higher the disappointment. So don't expect to get rich overnight and have a little patience.

What's the best choice to pick?

That depends on you. Individual choices vary and what works for one will not work for another. So don't choose an option just because someone else is choosing it. If you think the option will work well for you then pick it. Most people prefer to diversify their portfolio and have each of the elements in their choice of investments. You can do the same but don't rush into all of it. Take it slow and move to the next financial security only after you have fully exploited one option.

Can I quit anytime?

Yes. Starting and quitting is up to you. But don't quit when you have a lot of debt in the stock market. Quit only because you are satisfied with your investments. If you think you can create a lot of debts and run away from it then you will only get yourself into a lot of trouble. So don't be in a hurry to join and quit the stock market. Think out your decisions carefully and ensure that you know exactly what you are getting into.

These form the various questions that beginners ask about the stock market and I hope you had yours answered successfully.

Chapter 3: Stocks Basics

In the previous chapter, we looked at some questions and answers that will help you understand the topic of stock market better. In this chapter, we will read on the basics of stocks, their types and their various advantages and disadvantages to consider before choosing them.

What are they?

A stock is basically a share of the company. A share refers to a part of the company including its finances and every other asset that it owns. When the company decides to go public with its shares, it announces an IPO or initial public offering. Anybody interested in buying the shares will then approach the company and pay the share value to own the shares. This is known as primary selling. These shares are then sold in the share market. The share market is a huge place where buyers and sellers converge to conduct daily trade. These shares are then bought and sold and the seller capitalizes on the current price of the share, which will be much higher than what he had bought it at. The buyer will have the chance to capitalize on the share once its value rises.

Companies decide to go public with their shares due to many reasons. But the main reason is to raise capital for their business. So they will value their company and split the shares. They will then value individual shares depending on their market capture and asset to liability ratio. A small company might capture a big market share and a big company might capture a small share. It depends on the individual company's board members' decision.

So say A has 100 shares of Microsoft priced at $20 each. He will sell it to B who has to pay $2000 for it. Now B is holding on to it in a bid to sell it for $25 or $30 and make a profit on it.

The stock market is huge and there are many companies that list their shares. As an investor, you must choose the best one for yourself and invest wisely.

Types of stocks

Stocks are of two main types namely Common stock and Preferred stock. These types are different from each other and each one has a unique characteristic. You can choose either one after evaluating their meaning and characteristics.

Common stock

Also known as equity stocks, common stocks are what are mostly traded in the stock market. These are second hand stocks that the previous owners have pumped into the stock market. Common stock holders are generally placed at the bottom of the ownership staircase. They will be considered last if the time to payout comes by. So in case the company is winding up, these will be compensated last after the other stockholders have been paid in full. But these stocks are cheap and easily available and are ideal for short term trading. The only gain from these will be a dividend pay out or an earning from the difference in their share prices. Owners of this stock have the right to elect the board of members.

Preferred stocks

Preferred stocks are first hand stocks. These are considered first in case there is liquidation in the company. So it is a safe bet to buy such stocks. However, the holders have no right in electing the board of members in the company. But these stocks will help the holders avail a fixed rate of dividend regardless of the company undergoing profits or losses. So these stocks are much preferred.

These are the two types of shares available in the market and you can choose the best one depending on your analysis and needs.

Advantages of stocks

It is a good idea to invest in stocks, as there are many advantages to it. The first advantage is that you will avail a certain monthly income in the form of dividends that are paid out by the company. Although a single company will only pay once every quarter, you can hold stocks of as many companies as you like and have a consistent income. Another advantage is the choices that it gives you. You can either hold it for just a single day or hold it for years together. You don't have to dispose off what you buy immediately and can hold on to it if you think it will grow in value over time. Their liquidity is what makes them highly suited for both small and large investments. If you end up buying the stocks of a company that is on the verge of booming, then you will have the chance to be part owner of an extremely profitable company. Also, when you have your money invested in the stock market, you will not be able to withdraw from it easily. This is great for all those that have the habit of withdrawing money often and spending it unnecessarily.

Disadvantages of stocks

Just like the advantages, there are also certain disadvantages of investing in the stock market. The first one being volatility. As you know, the stock market is a very volatile place where the prices keep fluctuating every second. A good stock today might end up at the bottom of the pile tomorrow and your investment might get jeopardized. These stocks fluctuate owing to the demand and supply and it will be very difficult for you to predict these. In fact, what most stock investors find frustrating is how the prices can vary without any apparent reason and cause you losses. Another disadvantage is that it is not easy to get your hands on preferred stocks. So as common stock holders, you might not know everything that there is to about the company.

These form the various advantages and disadvantages of stocks and you can choose to invest in them if you think you have enough risk capital at your disposal.

Chapter 4: Bonds Basics

In the previous chapter, we read in detail about stocks, their types, advantages and disadvantages, in this chapter, we will do the same with Bonds.

What are they?

Bonds and stocks are often mentioned in the same breath but they differ drastically in terms of their structure and payouts. So comparing the two is wrong and will leave the investor confused.

Bonds are issues by companies to the public when they wish to raise money for their business. As you know, multi national companies will require a lot of capital for their day-to-day use and also to fund any new project. They will not always have this money readily available with them and will have to turn to other sources. Although there are many finance providing institutions such as banks and moneylenders, they will not be ready to finance a large amount of money.

So the best choice for these companies is to raise the money from the public. They will issue bonds to them for a fixed period of time after which they will pay out the entire sum borrowed along with a rate of interest. They might also agree to pay a monthly interest instead of paying it in lump sum. The value of the bond will be much lesser than its actual face value. So if the person wishes to dispose off the bond before its maturity then he will get paid a higher sum for it.

Bonds are said to be slightly more secure options as compared to stocks as there is no volatility. The pay out period is also pre determined so the person does not have to worry about holding on to the bonds for a long time.

Types of bonds

There are 5 main types of bonds and they are as follows:

Corporate bonds

As the name suggests, corporate bonds are issued by companies to the public. They will have to raise money for their company's projects and so, will issue bonds for the public. The public will then buy these by paying a certain amount of money. The company will promise to pay back the amount in say 2 years' time and in the meant time, pay a 10% interest on it. The main advantage of this type of investment is that, you will win over the company's loyalty. So they might end up issuing free shares to you at a low rate, which will allow you to become part owner of the company.

Government bonds

Government bonds are issued by the federal government. Just like the corporates, the government will also require money to fund its projects. And so, they will issue bonds to the public in a bid to raise money for themselves. You can buy these bonds and hold on to them until they reach their maturity period or dispose them off before that if you are in need of money. Even if you dispose them off, you will still get paid more than what you ha paid for them and you will transfer all your rights to the buyer of the bond.

Agency bonds

Agency bonds refer to those that are issued by affiliates of the government. So they are issued by those companies that are backed by the government but are not run by them. They will also issue bonds to raise money for their business. The same rules apply here as well where you can sell the bond to someone and get paid extra or hold on to it and earn a certain interest every month. Although these are backed by the government, they don't come with the same guarantees that government bonds come with. So ensure that you thoroughly read the terms and conditions first before investing in them!

Municipal bonds

Just like the federal government, the various local and state governments will also issue bonds to the public to raise money for its projects. These are also safe options to pick and you can earn a substantial rate of interest for your investment, which will be much higher than what your bank would pay you. Municipal bonds are some of the preferred types of bonds in the share market.

Zero coupon bonds

Zero coupon bonds are those that are valued much lesser than their actual value and the issued to you. After a while, they are bought back at their actual value. So if you bought a bond at $500, whose actual price is $800, you will get paid in full for it after 2 years. So you can realize a profit of $300 from it at a later date. These are safe options for you to pick for yourself.

Advantages of bonds

The main advantage of bonds is that, there are many guarantees attached to them. The first guarantee is that you will get back your money for sure, provided you invest in government bonds. The next guarantee is that you will receive a fixed rate of interest on your investment, which is extremely important for an investor. Bonds can be issued within a few minutes and you don't have to wait for too long for the investment to go through. These guarantees are not available with your share investments.

Disadvantages of bonds

The main disadvantage of bonds is the rate of return on your investment will not be as high as what the stock market will provide you. You will have to settle for a low rate and wait for years together before getting back your principle sum. The guarantees are always only associated with government bonds and you will not have any for your corporate and agency bonds. Even if they do pay you more than what the government bonds would, you will have to risk it all if you invest in corporate bonds.

These form the various advantages and disadvantages of investing in bonds and you can pick them depending on your needs and expectations from your investments.

You are halfway done!

Congratulations on making it to the halfway point of the journey. Many try and give up long before even getting to this point, so you are to be congratulated on this. You have shown that you are serious about getting better every day. I am also serious about improving my life, and helping others get better along the way. To do this I need your feedback. Click on the link below and take a moment to let me know how this book has helped you. If you feel there is something missing or something you would like to see differently, I would love to know about it. I want to ensure that as you and I improve, this book continues to improve as well. Thank you for taking the time to ensure that we are all getting the most from each other.

Chapter 5: ETFs, Options And Commodities Basics

By now, we have looked at stocks and bonds in detail. In this chapter, we will look at ETFs and options and understand the different concepts associated with them.

What are they?

Etfs stand for exchange transfer funds. These funds are a lot like mutual funds but are traded in the stock market. So a company will invest a part of their investment in different financial securities and then split up the investments into individual units. These are then bought and sold in the share market like regular stocks. But the difference is that you can buy and sell them on the same day as opposed to remaining invested in them for 3 to 5 years.

Types of ETFs

There are 6 main types of etfs that you can choose from and they are as follows.

Equity etfs

These etfs are those that will follow the pattern of the index. So, it will be a small sample of the index, like Amex, and you will possess a slice of the market when you buy yourself this etf.

Real estate etfs

As the name suggests, real estate etf is one where you will hold the shares of a company that invests in real estate projects. Since they are majorly being funded by the public, they will compulsorily have to declare 90% of their profits to the public. These are better known as Real estate Investment trusts and they are safe options for you to choose for your investments.

Currency etfs

These are foreign currency stocks. When you invest in these, you will be safeguarding your money against any inflation or deflation that might affect dollar value. You will also have the chance to make a foreign investment, which will diversify your portfolio. So these etfs are great for you.

Commodity etfs

Commodity etfs refer to those that are predominantly invested in the commodities market. So when you buy these, you will own a share in the commodities market but will not have to speculate and get dispose it off it, when it reaches your target price.

Fixed income etfs

These are better known as bond etfs. Here, you will receive a certain fixed rate of interest owing to owning etfs that correspond to bonds in the stock market.

Specialty etfs

These are special etfs that are formulated to help the investor avail a double or triple return on investment. These are also good choices for both beginners and old hands.

Advantages of ETFs

The main advantage of investing in etfs is that, they will provide you with the benefits of investing in mutual funds but give you the chance to trade them on a daily basis. So you can capture several different elements of the stock market at once and buy and sell them at the same time. The other advantage is risk diversification. By investing in etfs, you are diversifying your risk and are not investing in just one form of investment.

Disadvantages of ETFs

The disadvantage of etfs is that, you will not have the chance to make a lot of money on it and the rate of return on your investment will be very low. So, you might end up getting less than 5% return on your over all investment. Another disadvantage of etfs is that, they will move extremely slowly. They will move like snails and you will not be able to capitalize on their speed.

Options

Options, on the other hand, are schemes where you can reserve a financial security and not pay for them immediately. So say for example you wish to purchase a stock worth $50 and want 100 of them. Instead of paying $5000 for it, you tell the seller you will reserve the stock by paying $1000 for it. The seller will agree provided you pay in full within the agreed time period. Now say in a week's time, you realize that the stock belongs to a very good company and its value has risen to $60 per share. You can immediately pay the remaining money and buy the stock at the agreed price. The seller is forced to give it away at the lower price owing to his commitment.

On the other hand, suppose the price of the stock drops to $40 owing to internal issues in the company. You have agreed to pay $50 per share and if you are to sell it now, you will only get $40 for it. So here, you have the option to not pay in full at all and wipe your hands off of it. But you will have to lose the $1000 that you had paid as advance for it. This is still a good option, given how you will be saving $4000 on it.

Types of options

Options are of two main types viz. American options and European options

American options

American options are those that are extensively practiced in the market. This is a flexible option and is ideal for new and old investors. American options will give you the chance to sell your option at any time before the arrival of the maturity date. So you can encash on the stock's high price and sell it sometime before its maturity. So say for example you bought options of company A where you paid $500 as advance and wish to sell the stock for a $500 profit. The maturity date for the stock is 1 March 2016. If the opportunity presents itself for you to sell it on 1 October 2015 and realize a profit on it then you can take that option for yourself.

European options

European options are the next type of options that you can choose for yourself. These are not as flexible as American options, and are extremely rigid. They will only allow you to dispose them off after they have reached the maturity period. If in between you have the chance to capitalize on its value then you won't have the chance to do so. European options are not popular but they are available for you to choose.

Note: These are mere names for the options and have no geographic relevance.

Advantages of options

Options are great as the investment is quite safe. Even if you do end up losing the reservation money, you are still getting away with not paying the agreed amount. The rewards that options pay are high and possibly highest as compared to other forms of investments. Options are also easy to understand and operate and are ideal for beginners to understand how the stock market works.

Disadvantages of options

The major disadvantage of options is that it will be difficult to speculate. You will think the price will rise but it will end up falling and you will decide to pass on the date and not honor the deal and the price will rise up. So, it is difficult to understand when and how the prices of the security will rise and fall. Also, the reservation money will still be your hard earned money and having to lose it unnecessarily will hurt you financially.

Commodities

Commodities refer to everyday commodities that are bought and sold in the stock market. These are valued at a certain price and then you can sell them at a higher price. This is a form of speculative trade just like options trading. You can pick a certain commodity and then buy and sell it before its expiry date. Commodities trading are an advanced form of trading and you must take it up after careful evaluation.

Types of commodities

Energy: These are energies such as oil and gas. You will have to buy them at a certain price and then speculate on a future price. As soon as that price is reached, you can sell them. The difference will be your profit. These resources are rare and so, they will be priced highly.

Livestock: Livestock such as pig and chicken and meats such as pork are also traded in the market. You have to speculate on their price as well and then buy them. These are slightly less volatile and things such as weather conditions and market demand will affect them.

Metals: Metals such as iron, zinc and nickel are also traded. These are heavily used in industries and so; their market demand will be quite high. You must buy them at a certain price and then wait for their price to go up before selling them.

Agriculture: This is the most widely traded commodity in the market. Agricultural produce such as sugar, rice and vegetables are traded in the market. You will have to buy them in quintals to trade with them.

Advantages of commodities

The main advantage of investing in commodities is that, it is a safe option to invest in. Even during times of crisis, your commodities will remain safe and so will your investments. The returns that you earn from your commodities investments is also quite high, which is an added advantage. You can further diversify your business by investing in commodities. You must remain patient and understand the trade carefully to realize a profit on your investment.

Disadvantages of commodities

The main disadvantage of this form of investment is that, you will be willing to take a greater risk on your investment and end up creating losses for yourself. Another disadvantage is that the prices keep fluctuating too fast. So buy the time you decide to capitalize on a price, it would have shifted and you will end up losing money.

These for the various advantages and disadvantages of etfs, options and commodities and you must decide on one depending on your needs and capacity.

Chapter 6: Precious Metals And Foreign Exchange Basics

Stocks, bonds, etfs and options are all virtual securities. Apart from these, there are two other types that will give you a physical possession of your investments.

In this chapter, we will look at these two chapters in detail.

What are they?

Precious metals are gold, silver and platinum, which are traded in the stock market just like regular stocks. They are also valued at a certain price and traded in the bullion market. When you buy and sell these, you are looking to capitalize on its difference in value.

These metals are extensively used in the jewelry industry and also several other industries. This makes it extremely valuable and so, its prices keep going up and down all day long. So it is important to remain alert and observe the trends consistently and then invest in them.

Precious metals

Here are three of the most traded precious metals in the market

Gold: Gold as you know is extremely valuable. The yellow metal is used to make jewelry and also finds its use in the dental industry. You can either buy it in the form of coins or bars or also buy jewelry if you prefer that. But jewelry is not as valuable considering its weight will be less and the maker will charge you for its making. However, it cannot be ruled out as a good investment.

Silver: Silver is also a valuable precious metal. It finds its use in several industries. So the price will keep fluctuating all through the day. But the price per kg for silver is much lower than it is for gold and you can buy more of it.

Platinum: Platinum is the costliest of all precious metals. It is used in jewelry and many industries. Even with a large investment, you will only get a little platinum. So you have to buy it at the lowest price possible.

There is no time limit and you can hold these precious metals for as long as you like.

Advantages of precious metals

The main advantage of buying precious metals is that, you will get physical custody of your investment. Precious metals are extremely valuable and an investment here will be a safe option. You can sell your precious metals at any time and make money on it. Another advantage is that the prices will be global and you can exchange your precious metals for cash in any part of the world.

Disadvantages of precious metals

One disadvantage of buying precious metals is that, you will have to start with a big investment. Even so, you can only buy a little and make do with it. Remember that the higher the investment, the higher the return.

Foreign currencies

Foreign currencies are exchanged just as precious metals. Each of these currencies has a certain value, which will be higher or lower when compared to other currencies. When you buy the currencies of one country, you can exchange it for another countries currency and come into a profit.

Advantages of foreign currencies

The main advantage of buying and selling foreign currencies is that, the market is extremely big and you can capitalize on its diversity. You can buy and sell many currencies on the same day.

Disadvantages of foreign currencies

The disadvantage of dealing in foreign currencies is that, you have to adjust to the other countries times if you want to trade consistently.

Chapter 7: Money Management Tips

As you know, it is not enough for you to understand the basics of investing and must know to manage it properly. You cannot keep investing unless you have enough money saved up for yourself.

So to educate you on matters of money management, we will look at some things that you must do today!

Budgeting

Preparing a budget is extremely important. A budget is meant to help you keep track of your incomes and expenses. When you track these, you know whether you are spending properly or are over spending your money.

The basics of a budget involve recording your incomes on one side and your expenses on the other. Draw out a table and mention all the incomes on one side and the expenses on the other. Now tally both and see which one is higher. If the incomes are higher then you are left with a surplus and if the expense total is higher, then you have a deficit.

It is important for you to always have a surplus as that means you are spending less than what you are making. This surplus can be saved. But if you have a deficit, then you will have to reduce it and try and match your expenses and incomes. Then you further cut down on unnecessary expenditures and create a surplus.

Saving

Saving money is the second step that you must take towards managing your money efficiently. You cannot invest if you don't have savings. So before getting into the stock market, make sure you have enough money saved up with you. These savings can be in the form of bank deposits or bonds. Both of them will return your money back to you after attaching a certain interest. But you must choose places that offer you good rate of interest. Decide on a number, like $10,000 and ensure that your savings reach that mark. Only then should you decide to start investing your money in the market.

I know it is easier said than done, as not everybody will have the motivation to save money. So the best thing to do is reward yourself every time you put money into the savings account. Mind you, this should be surplus money that will only supplement whatever money you have decided to directly transfer from your checking account to your savings account on a monthly basis. If you have a spouse or a partner then ask them to do the same.

Safe investments

When it comes to savings, ensure that you trust only reliable sources. Many people decide to trust frauds and end up losing their hard earned money. There will be several fraudsters and scammers out there who will prey on innocent victims and dupe them. They will not appear to be scammers and will look extremely innocent. You have to be wary of such people and stay as away from their fraudulent schemes. Even if it is a colleague or someone you know, don't enter any scheme without conducting due research.

Trading

When it comes to trading in the stock market, you have to be very careful. You must not make silly mistakes, which will cause you to lose money instead of gaining. Losing money is never an option and you must put in all efforts to increase your money's worth. Don't be over enthusiastic and plan everything out in advance. Come up with a plan of action to follow. Stick to your plan and don't deviate from it. You can take the help of a friend to plan out your finances and then invest it in all the best places.

Retirement planning

Remember that you must plan for your retirement. You must have enough money saved up to lead a comfortable life. You must not depend on others for your financial needs. Start with a plan and follow through with it. You must also contribute towards your 401(k). Have your own house and your own car as well. These are basic things but you must pay attention to them if you wish to retire in peace.

These form just some of the money management tips for you to follow but are not limited to just these.

Chapter 8: Trading Tips

In the previous chapter, we looked at some money management tips for you. It is important that you manage your money in the best possible way and understand the value of increasing its potential over time.

Learn daily

The stock market is a place where every day new stories are made. If you think you have seen it all, then you are absolutely wrong! Treat every day as a new day and every incident as a learning curve to take away a lesson from it. What you learn today will benefit you tomorrow and so on and so forth. Don't assume things for yourself and make a note of all the incidents that you face. Even if it is a bad situation, learn to take a lesson from it. It might be a temporary phase but you must consider it a threat at all times.

Invest risk capital

When it comes to stock market investments, remember that you are investing real money that you will have to risk. So, invest whatever you are willing to lose. Better known as risk capital, you have to calculate your risk and know exactly how much you might end up losing in the market. It's obvious that you will not always lose the money but it is best to be prepared for the worst. Another piece of advice is to always invest your own money and not somebody else's money. Even if someone willfully gives you the money to spend, you will still be responsible for it and it will be impossible for you to predict the future and your stocks might end up crashing which is a very big risk.

Own mind

Remember to always have your own mind when it comes to investing in the stock market. If you rely too much on others for their advice and opinions, then you will end up making mistakes. You will have two opinions to work with and remain confused all the time. So don't trust others too much and simply consider their opinion once. When you hear about a good stock, do your own research for it instead of blindly trusting the news. Many times, the news will turn out to be a hoax. So be careful and not blindly trust everything you hear from others, everybody if they are experts.

Be prepared

When it comes to the stock market, you have to mentally prepare for it. Remain ready to take a loss on some of the stocks, as you cannot always remain in profit. The best thing to do is maintain a 5% loss risk in all stocks and not any more. You will have to make use of a technique known as stop loss, where you decide how much loss you can take on a stock. Don't worry if you take loss on a few stocks in a row. It's just an indication that you should take it slow and start trading wisely. You will know to invest wisely and not make the same mistakes over and over again.

Diversify

Diversification is an extremely important part of your stock market investments. When you diversify, you spread out your risk and profit. If you invest everything in the same place, you have to settle for anything that it offers you regardless of good or bad. But if you spread your risk, then you will have to bear only a little and your other investments can save you. Many beginners make the mistake of investing in just one type of security and don't consider diversifying. But you don't make that mistake and try to maintain as diverse a portfolio as possible.

Timing

Timing the market is essential. There are clear times when it will be best to buy a security and hold it and times when it will be good to sell them. You have to understand the difference in the timings and invest wisely. Don't be in a hurry to make the decisions. Nobody is asking you to buy and sell within a few seconds. Take your time to analyze and assess a situation before making a decision. It will be a little difficult in the beginning but nothing that you cannot learn to do.

Understand brokerage

Remember that it is a compulsion for you to sign up with a brokering firm to trade in the stock market. If you don't, then you cannot trade at all. So find the best firm for yourself and ensure that you pay only a little towards them as the commission. Many people end up paying a lot of money as commission, which eats away into their profits. So check the rate of commission first and then sign up with them. You will avoid a lot of unnecessary arguments and problems by doing so.

No love

Remember to never get too attached with a financial security. People end up falling in love with a company and refuse to let go of their stocks. Similarly, they will get attached to gold and not wish to sell it even if a lucrative offer comes by. So leave love and emotions out of it and focus only on your profits and losses. You have to remain mentally and emotionally strong and remain as away from establishing a bonding as possible with all your stocks.

Penny stocks

Penny stocks refer to those stocks that are valued at less than $5. These stocks are said to be good investments but only if you know to trade in them. Don't buy them if you don't know how to trade intraday. They will rise and fall within a single day and you have to be quick in making your decisions. Penny stocks can make you rich and poor in a matter of seconds and so, you have to invest in them only if you have the confidence to handle their volatility.

Expectations

It is obvious that you will have certain expectations from your stock market investments. Some will have high expectations and some will have low. But it is best to find a middle path and have limited expectations out of it. These should not be too high or too low and must lie somewhere in between.

These form the different trading tips that you must understand and incorporate to make the most of your investments.

Key Takeaways

When you wish to invest in the stock market, you have to start with the very basics. You cannot simply jump into it without knowing anything about it. Start by understanding how the stock market operates and acquaint yourself with all the different terms that are used in the trade. These details will help make your stock market journey easier.

Understanding the different risks that the stock market throws at you is important to know. Remember that no investment guarantees anything and you have to be prepared for the worst. But don't get scared, it is only a precautionary measure and it is best to calculate your risk when you wish to invest money in the stock market.

Stocks are the first type of investments to consider. Stocks are shares of the company and when someone buys them, they own a part of the company. These shares are listed in the stock market and are bought and sold on a daily basis. You can indulge in intraday trading or long-term investments.

Bonds are the next choice that you can pick. Bonds are issued by governments or corporates and you can buy them at a lower face value and sell them at a higher price. The best way to pick bonds is by going by recommendations. You can invest in them for a year or more and it is best suited for those looking for consistent returns.

Etfs are like mutual funds but traded on the stock market. You can buy and sell them on a daily basis and capitalize on its price difference. Etfs are generally slow moving so you will have to wait for it to rise in value over a period of time. But don't give up on them too early as once they begin to pick up speed, you can capitalize on it.

Options are investments that will allow you to stick with your deal or walk away from it. So you can choose to either stay put with your commitment or walk away from it. But there is a catch. You will have to pay a certain sum as a reservation amount and will have to let go of it if you wish to walk away from the deal. So you need to be careful while picking options.

Commodities are traded on the market every day. There are metals, livestock, agricultural products and energy resources, which are listed in the market. You can buy them at a certain price and then sell them when they increase in value. Commodities help you diversify your portfolio.

Precious metals are like commodities except that you can get physical possession after buying them. Here too, you must capitalize on their price variations. You can hold on to your precious metals for as long as you like.

Foreign currencies are also traded on a daily basis. One country's currency will always be lesser or higher in value as compared to another country's currency. You must capitalize on this difference to earn from it.

Managing money is extremely important. It is not enough if you investment money. You have to start with savings. Prepare a monthly budget and devise a savings plan. Once you have enough savings, you can start investing.

When you enter the stock market, take it slow and don't be in a hurry to make money. If you go too fast then you will end up making unnecessary mistakes. Make use of precautionary measures to safeguard your investments.

Conclusion

I thank you once again for choosing this book and hope you had a good time reading it.

The main aim of this book was to educate you on the basics of the stock market. As you can see, there are many things to learn, and understand, before you start investing in the stock market. But once you understand these thoroughly, you will be able to invest and realize a profit on your capital investments.

The next step is for you to incorporate these ideals and start investing your money in the stock market and hope you find success.

All the best!

Free membership into the Mastermind Self Development Group!

For a limited time, you can join the Mastermind Self Development Group for free! You will receive videos and articles from top authorities in self development as well as a special group only offers on new books and training programs. There will also be a monthly member only draw that gives you a chance to win any book from your Kindle wish list!

If you sign up through this link http://www.mastermindselfdevelopment.com/specialreport you will also get a special free report on the Wheel of Life. This report will give you a visual look at your current life and then take you through a series of exercises that will help you plan what your perfect life looks like. The workbook does not end there; we then take you through a process to help you plan how to achieve that perfect life. The process is very powerful and has the potential to change your life forever. Join the group now and start to change your life! http://www.mastermindselfdevelopment.com/specialreport

Real Estate Investing

Free membership into the Mastermind Self Development Group!

For a limited time, you can join the Mastermind Self Development Group for free! You will receive videos and articles from top authorities in self development as well as a special group only offers on new books and training programs. There will also be a monthly member only draw that gives you a chance to win any book from your Kindle wish list!

If you sign up through this link http://www.mastermindselfdevelopment.com/specialreport you will also get a special free report on the Wheel of Life. This report will give you a visual look at your current life and then take you through a series of exercises that will help you plan what your perfect life looks like. The workbook does not end there; we then take you through a process to help you plan how to achieve that perfect life. The process is very powerful and has the potential to change your life forever. Join the group now and start to change your life! http://www.mastermindselfdevelopment.com/specialreport

Table of Contents

Exposure

Illiquidity

Calamities

Bad tenants

Foreign investors

Chapter 4: Tips For Beginners

Do your reading

No expertise required

Understand language

Save up

Know your numbers

Have a plan

Consult

Start small

Keep track

Sell, buy

Chapter 5: Types Of Real Estate Properties

Residential real estate properties

Commercial real estate properties

Industrial real estate properties

Retail real estate properties

Mixed properties

Foreign properties

Miscellaneous

   Construction

   Container homes

   Recreational properties

Chapter 6: Mistakes To Avoid While Real Estate Investing

Paying too much

Looking without money

Not doing research

Not liking property

Assuming things

Doing everything by yourself

Miscalculating

Time frame

One exit strategy

Trusting agents

Chapter 7: Real Estate Finance Sources

Bank loans

Credit unions

Life insurance corporations

Mortgage brokers

Finance companies

Pension funds

REITS

Foreign funds

Government schemes

Individual Investors

Relatives

Places to look for real estate

    Online

    Classifieds

    Clubs / Unions

    Agents

Key Highlights

Conclusion

Introduction

When it comes to investing, there are many options to choose from. Right from buying stocks and bonds to precious metals and business investments, the options seem never ending. But one option, out of all these, makes for a great choice for both beginners and profound investors. That option is known as Real Estate Investments.

Real estate investments are great investment choices for everybody, as they are meant to help diversify your portfolio, and also provide you a sense of security. But it is easier said than done to own a property, as there will be a million things to consider before buying a house or an apartment.

To make it easier for you, this book will act as your real estate investment guide and help you make the right choice for yourself.

It contains proven steps and strategies that help you buy and sell properties with ease, in the US.

Let us start.

Chapter 1: FAQs On the Subject

First and foremost, I wish to thank you for choosing this book and hope you have a good time reading it. In this first chapter of the book, I will ask and answer a few basic questions on the topic, to help you understand it better.

What is real estate investment?

Real estate investment refers to the buying of a property, which can be a house or an apartment, or just a piece of land meant to be converted into property. Real estate investments have existed since time immemorial as everybody needs a roof over their head, and it feels great if you own the place you live in. Also, if you buy yourself a retail outlet or an industrial establishment and rent it out, then that will also be counted as a real estate investment. So, the term has a very broad meaning and anything that involves the buying of property can be termed as a real estate investment.

Purchasing a home to dwell in permanently as opposed to renting it out or using it as a form of passive income is the difference between a purchase and an investment. You want your real estate property to ultimately make you money so you will be looking for different things in a home than you would be if you were looking for a home to purchase for yourself or your family. Investing in real estate is one of the best options for the long-term for a variety of reasons, all of which will be discussed in the coming sections and chapters. Investing needs to be done with the intent to make money, legally and efficiently.

Is real estate a good investment?

Yes. Real estate is a great investment choice. Arguably one of the best forms of investment, purchasing real estate not only gives you ownership of the home or dwelling but also to the land beneath. There are many investment options out there, but real estate is seen as a good choice owing to the several benefits it offers. Right from first-time investors to those who already have a few investments made, real estate is a smart choice for anyone looking to diversify their portfolio. As a beginner, you will obviously have your doubts on its true benefits, but through the course of this book, you will understand exactly how beneficial real estate investments can be and why it is a great idea for you to invest in.

There are a lot of questions surrounding why real estate is considered a good investment by some and a terrible investment by others. You are at risk, should there be another housing collapse...however if you are choosing to rent the property out, this won't affect you nearly as negatively if you were attempting to remodel and sell the property. Even if the home depreciates in value due to economy or age, you still have the land with which the home lives on. Land will only continue to increase in value over time. Real estate is a lifelong investment with lifelong advantages. There are disadvantages that we will cover in the coming chapters.

Can it be part of my portfolio?

Yes. Real estate can be a part of your portfolio. Anytime you are obtaining income from something you purchased; this can go in your financial portfolio. Although any income you derive from it will fall under the passive income category, your investment in itself will be counted as a portfolio investment. There are many types of portfolio investments, no doubt, but real estate can be seen as a very stable and reliable portfolio investment that will aid in stabilizing your overall investments. Most investors will look to real estate as a diversification option and one that will allow them to invest a lot of money in one go.

Real estate is looked favorably upon because there is no question whether or not the value will either increase or decrease. We already know land will increase in value in the coming decades even if the home falls to pieces so that alone makes for a positive, passive income on your portfolio. Portfolios should always be kept up to date so making sure you have the correct stats and numbers is crucial if you are looking for help from investors. Investors tend to look favorably upon real estate investments in portfolios.

What is REIT?

REIT stands for real estate investment trust and is a security that is traded on the stock exchange. It helps in directly investing in real estate properties and allows you to own a property in a short period of time. When you buy a REIT, then you will be contributing towards buying a property that is traded in the exchange. These REITs are funded by the rents that they receive from these properties. You can buy them directly from a stock exchange or indirectly through a mutual fund. You can combine it with a dividend reinvestment plan.

In other words, real estate investing trusts are companies that own properties that produce income (income producing properties). Within these trusts (companies), they own a variety of different real estate that produces income either residentially or commercially and can range from hospitals to warehouses to hair salons. As long as the property generates incomes, it can be within the real estate investing trust. They are originally derived from mutual funds, and they allow you to generate income from purchasing stocks as opposed to the entire property. Real estate investment trusts can be formed or joined; forming one requires that your business meets strict financial and organizational standards, numbers and regulations to be considered eligible.

Who is the best candidate to invest in real estate?

Anybody interested in buying a property for themselves can invest in real estate. Anybody who has enough resources to buy a property is an ideal candidate to invest. Minors will need the approval of an adult to buy properties in their name. But individuals to partners and spouses can all invest in real estate. If you are already an active investor in stocks and other financial securities, then you will not find it tough to invest in real estate. You will already have proper knowledge on the subject and will need just a little nudge to get going. Keep in mind, never invest more than you can afford. If you purchase a property with the intent on renting it immediately, make sure you have at least 6 months' rent (mortgage payments) in your savings in case of unforeseen circumstance or inability to rent. You don't want to purchase the property and default on the payments shortly after because you didn't plan accordingly.

As far as ultimately deciding if one person is a good enough candidate for real estate or not depends on the person's drive and ambition. Someone who doesn't have enough money to fund a maintenance man for properties, better have knowledge of hardware and basic maintenance in order to save money by doing the work himself. This also goes for renovating and remodeling the inside and outside of the property. Many people write off real estate investing because they assume they won't be able to afford it however most people don't realize that a lot of work on homes can be done by the homeowners themselves. Candidacy for real estate investing lies solely in the drive of the purchaser (or investor) and should never be written off without subsequent research and networking.

How much money should I invest?

Investment depends on the type of investment you wish to make, the size and the length of the investment. The final decision of how much money will be pooled into buying your property will depend on you. You have to make sure you have money to not just buy a property but also fix it up if necessary or make some changes. So it is important to have all your investments mapped out and know exactly how much needs to go where. Some places or builders will require you to make a minimum investment, and you will have to find out about it before buying a property. Keeping a budget and sticking to it is incredibly important and crucial in your financial welfare. Allot a certain amount of money for each project and shuffle the money around accordingly if one project is cheaper or more expensive than initially estimated.

Determining the amount to invest should also be done before the purchase of the home. Are you looking to spend a quarter of a million on a home? Or are you looking for a cheap, fixer upper under 90K? Regardless, you are going to need to budget and determine the total amount you need to invest in order to get the highest rate on your return in the shortest possible time. If the return on your investment isn't going to happen in your lifetime, you should probably look elsewhere. This also goes for properties that don't make more than 100 a month – these can be more of a hassle than they are worth. Plan wisely and stick to your budget for purchasing and investing.

How long should the investments be made?

That depends on you. You can make an investment for as long as you like. Generally, when people buy houses, they hold it for a minimum of 5 years to avail tax benefits and other such monetary benefits. But you can choose any time period you like. Most people will have an emotional attachment towards the first house that they buy and will not part with it for several years in a row. So for that sake, you will have to make a great initial investment and hold on to it for at least a decade or so.

The length of your investment can also be determined by the amount of money you are able to borrow and the amount you want to pay monthly on your mortgage. The less you are obligated to pay monthly, the more you can pay additionally each month to go toward the principle amount instead of interest. For example, say your mortgage is $400 a month, but you can afford $800 – make your $400 payment and then an additional $400 to go towards the total amount owed, not the interest. With the $400 payment, around $60 or so is going to interest. Whereas if you were paying a mortgage of $800, over $100 would be going toward interest and you wouldn't be able to put any additional money towards the principle.

What options do I have after investing?

After you buy the property, you have two main choices. The first being, moving in and occupying your property and living there for as long as you like! And the second is to rent out your property to someone. Both are good choices for you and the second one might give you a bigger advantage owing to receiving a rent on your investment. You also have the option to make a relative stay in your house as a caretaker, if you don't want the hassles of tenants. But that will not provide you with any form of monetary benefits. A third option (though not as relevant) would be to purchase the property, fix it up, and sell it for higher than you purchased. This option allows you to make a profit in a lump sum as opposed to monthly payments from tenants, but it is also very risky. More on these options in later sections.

Determining what you do with your property initially will depend on the financial situation you are in. Some people choose to dwell in their new home for a year or so before looking elsewhere and renting out their home. Other people choose to rent it out right away, never entertaining the idea of occupying the space. Some people end their rental agreements after the lease is up and decide they don't want to rent it anymore; they would like to live in it either full or part time. The options are endless in terms of flexibility. Granted, you shouldn't have rented to tenants who plan on making the home theirs for 10 years, only to kick them out after their initial one-year lease is up because you changed your mind and want to live there. It does not work like that. You are renting out your home to another person so they can have a home. Legally, you can't take it from them without a significant amount of notice and ethically, you shouldn't take it if they are wonderful tenants who plan on residing there for an extended period of time.

Is the income taxable?

Yes. The income that you receive in the form of rent or lease from the property is taxable. The tax will depend on how much you earn from the investment. If you earn a big sum as rent, then you will be taxed accordingly. You will have to go through the tax manual to understand it clearly. But even if you are taxed it will be just a small percentage of what you earn. The best thing to do is account for the tax that will be deducted and then set a rental price. That way, you don't lose out on any profit that you make from your investment. Many real estate investors take a certain percentage out of every rent payment they receive to allot to taxes at the end of the year. Once you have been in business for a few years, you will get a better idea of how much taxes you will be paying at the end of the year. The first few years it is wise to over save to avoid not being able to pay taxes at the end of the year.

Most of the time, if not always, income that you receive that is not taxed in itself, will be taxable income. For example, when a tenant writes you a rent check with their own personal checkbook, taxes aren't calculated. It is a set fee due by them per their contract every month, no taxes included. This way, it is your responsibility as the landlord to pay taxes on all your rental income received per the law. Failure to pay your tax could result in fines, wage garnishment and if done for a long enough period of time, jail time. It is imperative that you keep track of every payment received and every dollar spent. A great way to do this is to set up a filing system and stick to it strictly.

Are there risks involved?

Yes. As is with any investment, there is a certain amount of risk involved in real estate investments. The degree of risk will vary according to the type of investment that you make. If you are looking for a big condo or a villa, then the risk will be slightly higher, but your gain from it will also be high. If you are looking for a small house or an apartment, then your risk will be lower and so will your returns from it. So your risk and reward can be directly proportional. However, there can be cases where you buy an apartment at a posh locality for a low price and end up making a huge profit on it. So the risk is only subjective and will vary from investment to investment. There are ways to reduce your risk, though real estate in itself has always had a slight degree of risk. Make decisions based on facts and numbers, not on emotion. Don't make any decision without thinking on it for a few days. Always be frugal; money can be a curse and a blessing so it needs to be used wisely, not carelessly.

You have to look at an investment as a risk. Although every aspect of life takes risks, real estate investments can be a huge financial risk if you aren't smart with your money and you don't do your research. For example, you don't want to purchase a commercial office space with the intent on renting it out in a strip mall that only has ¼ of the space occupied due to economic downturn. A good example would be to purchase a large home with several bedrooms near a college and rent out the rooms to college students. You have to know the location and if you don't, research, research, research. You can minimize your risk significantly if you simply put in the effort to research every variable in the market.

How long before I get keys to a property?

It will depend on the type of investment that you make. Generally, it can take one month to a few months depending on the seller of the property. It will also take some time for your credit to be approved by a financial institution. So you will have to wait for some time before you possess the keys to your house and if there is a way to expedite the process, then you can exploit it.

For the most part, it is nearly impossible to tell when you will get the keys to your place. If you communicate with the original owners regularly, you may be able to get the keys sooner. If you have never met the previous owners and the real estate company has the keys, you will likely have to wait longer.

The waiting period also depends on the type of sale – short sale, foreclosure, auction or basic sale. Short sales tend to take significantly longer to process due to the paperwork and loopholes involved. Many people stray away from short sales for this particular reason. In any event, you will eventually get the keys to your new place and be able to move in.

These form some of the basic questions on real estate investments and hope you had yours answered.

Chapter 2: Advantages of Real Estate Investing

When it comes to real estate investing, there are many advantages that come with it. In this chapter, we will look at some of the most important advantages that real estate investments bring with them.

Monetary benefit

The main advantage of real estate investments is the monetary benefits that they give to the investor. When you buy a house and rent it out, then you earn money from it. Although you might not be able to use all the money that you get from it, you might still be left with a sizable sum. Say for example you get $500 from your apartment and pay $300 towards the mortgage. You will still be left with $200, which is your profit. After a while, when you are debt free, you will have full access to the rent that you receive.

When you initially purchase a home, it can quickly go to your head when you earn a profit in a way that appears to be so incredibly simple. However, should anything go wrong on the property, you are going to be liable. You never know when you will get the call about a broken window or air conditioner. Due to this constant risk, you need to put money aside for whatever emergency repairs may need to be done. When you initially start to churn a profit, you need to make sure you put a large percentage of that money in a savings account so you can make any necessary repairs on the house as quickly as possible. As a landlord, you are obligated to ensure that property is livable within the guidelines and regulations. Using your initial monetary benefit to make sure this is possible will give you peace of mind.

Borrowing money

When it comes to real estate investments, it will be easy for you to borrow money in the form of credit. Now suppose you wish to borrow $10,000 for a house, the credit institution will be more than happy to give it to you because they think of property or real estate investments as safe bets. But if you were to need the same money for any other reason, then the institution would refrain from lending you the money. So it is an easy task to finance your real estate investment.

It is important never to borrow more than you need. The more you borrow, the more you will owe in the long run because the higher the loan, the higher the interest accumulation. Borrowing money should only be done with you have exhausted all other options and you know you will be financially stable enough to pay back the loan in the long run. Don't make the mistake of taking a loan as a high-risk individual and a high-interest rate, only to lose your day job and no longer be able to make the mortgage payments. You may need to borrow money multiple times if you are planning on making real estate investing your full-time profession.

Parallel income

Your real estate investment can be a source of parallel income. In this day and age where nothing suffices, including your monthly income, you will have the chance to use your investment to earn a supplementary income. This will be known as passive income and you will not have to do anything to earn it. The money will keep flowing into your account on a monthly basis, and all you have to do is supervise the tenant. If you lease it out, then it is hassle free, and you can place the amount in a bank and earn interest on the sum of money.

This is one of the greatest parts about owning rental property. You have residual or passive income that consistently flows in (unless you are plagued with awful tenants), and with money you can use as additional investment money, place into an account that gains interest over time, or spend it carelessly (just kidding about the last part). There is a multitude of reasons why having a source of parallel income is not only financially rewarding; it also gives you a sense of financial security in case something should happen in the future. Save your passive income and spend it wisely. You never know when you an emergency might happen.

Tax benefit

There is a lot of tax benefit to be availed from your real estate investment. You can save money when you buy a property for yourself. This money can be saved both when you buy the property and when you renovate it. So you can avail dual benefits from your property investment. To understand the true tax benefit that you can avail from your property, please refer to the tax benefit on property investments website.

Your specific property or real estate tax benefit will vary depending on the state you are in, so do your own research to find out if the benefit does apply to you. Usually, landlords are responsible for paying taxes on income from rental properties but during renovations and initial purchasing, there may be some fees you can write off if the real estate is part of your business.

Appreciation

When you buy a property, it will not always be valued at the same rate. This means that it will grow in value over time. Many things will determine the appreciation including the locality of the property, the amenities that surround it, the neighborhood, etc. With time, your small investment will grow in tremendous value and give you a great rate of interest on your investment. In fact, it will give you a rate that no other form of investment will give you including share market investments. It is ideal to assume a 10% appreciation on a monthly basis. You want to avoid the opposite of appreciation which is depreciation; allowing the value of your real estate purchase to devalue over time by not maintaining the property and doing necessary renovations.

It is fairly easy to have your property appreciate over time. There are factors outside of your control and within your control to ensure your home maintains its value and ultimately appreciates. For example, a landlord or homeowner can do nothing to stop the housing collapse, but they can do necessary inspections, repairs, remodeling and renovations to make sure their home is safe, livable and new. This can require a great deal of expense initially, but regular inspections will ensure your home is up to date and can prevent major problems from damage that that goes unsolved for long periods of time.

Retirement benefits

A real estate investment is an automatic retirement investment. All you have to do is buy yourself a house or two and your retirement is secure. You can move into your house after you retire or rent it out to avail a consistent cash flow. You will not have to worry about your income coming to a halt and continue to lead the lifestyle you led when you were earning an income. So a real estate investment is a great opportunity for you to secure your retirement and not have to depend on others for money.

The benefits of having residual income during retirement speaks for itself. Now a days, many retirees find it difficult to afford their bills alone, keeping them from enjoying their retirement years with travel and fun. With residual income, you can enjoy your retirement years by having your pension or retirement from a job, social security and income from your real estate properties. Just an extra few hundred a month can make all the difference in the world when it comes to paying bills and saving for traveling. People look forward to retirement, but if you don't have the money to do anything during retirement, then it can become miserable. Plan accordingly and most importantly, plan ahead!

Security

Having a house is seen as a great confidence booster. Unlike investing in other avenues such as a business, it is a great idea to invest in real estate. The sense of security is deepened when you move into your house or get possession of the keys. You will develop a sense of security and not have to worry about not having a place to live in. once you make one real estate investment, you will develop the confidence to make another one and so on. You can keep going until such time as you have amassed a sizeable real estate collection. One of the hardest parts in real estate investment is actually taking that step to follow through. Once you go through the process and realize you can do it, you will likely do it again. It can take a lot of willpower to follow through with your commitment, but when you do, the results are astounding.

Once you obtain the real estate property and continually obtain rental payments, the financial security that follows is impenetrable. Being a landlord and being self-employed is empowering all on its own but also being able to provide a family with housing in exchange for rental payments is even more empowering.

Physical possession

It is important to take physical possession of an investment as it heightens your confidence and improves your mental and emotional state. This is not possible on the stock exchanges where you cannot really own a company by buying its shares. Real estate investment is a lot like precious metal investment where you can actually touch and feel whatever you have invested in. Once you move into your house, your sense of pride and confidence will only surge, and you will consider it as the best investment that you made in your life.

Sometimes, just being handed the keys is enough to bring someone to tears. Obtaining a home or investment of your own is a huge step in someone's life and the emotions attached are only natural. An unarguable fact about real estate investment is that you can touch and feel your investment. For example, stocks are merely words attached with worth. You can't hold them and touch them whereas with your real estate investment you can physically touch the home and feel it. It's a difficult thing to describe to someone who is used to the digital, technological side of investing and purchasing. With real estate, it's almost ancestral to be able to stand on land that you own and know that it is yours.

Protection

Unlike stocks and shares, you have the chance to protect your real estate investment. This means that you take up an insurance cover and protect your house. You will not have to worry about anything happening to your house. You can kick back and relax and allow your insurance to help protect your investment. You can also do other physical things like employing security to safe guard your investment, which is not possible in the stock market or any other form of investment.

Different states have different types of insurance that you may want to look into. There is flood insurance, hurricane insurance, renter's insurance, and homeowner's insurance 1 and 2. Pay attention to your policy and know what is covered. Roof damage is usually covered by homeowner's insurance but only if the roof is under a certain age. Same goes for flooding; insurance won't cover septic flood damage if you neglected to get regular inspections and make sure your septic tank was up to date. There are a lot of loopholes you need to tie down to make sure you don't pay out of pocket for expenses that could have been covered if you had paid more attention.

Inflation benefit

You will still have your house in times of inflation. Almost every other form of investment will be adversely affected by inflation except your property investment. So even if prices are flaring up, you will always have your property to fall back on. If you live in a big house, then you can consider moving into a smaller one and renting out your big place to have some extra money coming in until such time as the inflation has passed. You can move back once the economy has stabilized or remain put to receive the money consistently. Inflation is a real concern in today's society although it isn't increasing nearly as rapidly as originally thought.

These form just some of the advantages of real estate investments, but it is not limited to just these. You will have the chance to realize the other benefits once you buy your own property.

Chapter 3: Disadvantages of Real Estate Investments

Just like the various advantages, there will be several disadvantages to owning property, or making a real estate investment. It would be unfair for us to look at just the advantages, and we will also have to know the disadvantages to get a clear picture.

In this chapter, we will look at the disadvantages of real estate investments that you must know about before you make an investment.

Depreciation

Just like appreciation, there will be a little depreciation in the value of the property. It is important to consider this as the property will age and that will cause its value to slightly come down. You cannot expect your house to simply be appreciated and not be depreciated. If you take it as a 10% appreciation a year, then you must consider 2% depreciation as well. This will leave you with an 8% appreciation a year, which is not bad. So you have to consider both the appreciation and the depreciation to know your property's true worth.

Depreciation can happen when properties aren't maintained properly. For example, your air conditioning unit filter isn't changed regularly, so your air conditioner begins to freeze up. Over time, your HVAC system is being overworked, and its life expectancy and reliability drops significantly. Due to this, you will either have to prematurely replace your HVAC system or go without. A home with air conditioning, heating and ventilation are essentially valueless and uninhabitable. Proper maintenance and inspections can catch issues before they become expense or damage the home. There are cases where depreciation is out of our control and in this case, do everything you can on your end to lessen the blow financially...or sit on the property until the land appreciates.

Upkeep

The upkeep of a property can prove to be a headache. There will be a million things to take care of and look into when you buy a property. Apart from the apartment or house, you will also have to take care of the outsides and the surroundings. You will have to look into security installments and safeguard your house. You must also ensure that the wear and tear of the house is looked after and that nothing is damaging your property. All in all, there will be a million things for you to consider when you buy a property or yourself and you have to be on your feet if you want to safeguard it for a long time.

Upkeep falls parallel to preventing depreciation of your home. Upkeep is important to the home and the tenant's well-being. Unhappy tenants won't take care of a home that their landlord doesn't seem to care about. Upkeep needs to involve a combination of tenants (changing AC filters, cutting the grass, vacuuming and regular cleaning chores) and by the landlord (inspections, maintenance, lawn maintenance if applicable, and quick response to work orders by tenants. Keeping the home's value and livability falls in line with upkeep and a home's simply won't increase if the home is not cared for. As landlords treat the home as if it were your own – the same goes for tenants.

Ideal property

It is very tough to find an ideal property or a property of your dreams. You will have to hunt day and night to find something that you like. It will be tough to find something that suits all your requirements. You will have to scour for the best price, the best property, the best location and the best value for money. Such projects are hard to come by, and it will take very long for you to find the ideal property. Yu will have to employ a real estate agent if you wish to expedite the process but they will sometimes add to your woes.

Many of us are at odds about what exactly the ideal property consists of. Some of us want a large, older home near a college campus so they can rent out rooms for short terms. Some people want a decent, family sized home that they can rent to a family for an extended period of time, and others want a larger apartment building so they can have multiple families dwelling and paying rent. The ideal property is most often associated with an ideal location, and the ideal location varies from state to state. Southeast states may long for Atlantic Ocean views whereas the Midwest longs for mountain, lake and prairie views. New York City's ideal location is in the center of town where everything is easily accessible by walking whereas some people prefer to drive or take a longer walk to where they are going. Some people prefer quiet, and some prefer noise, like I said, it depends on the person.

Bad credit

If you have bad credit, then borrowing money for your investment will be very tough. You will have to convince the credit institution to lend you credit for your investment. This can be a herculean task and even if it does get approved, you will have to pay a big rate of interest on it. So it will be a bad situation if you borrow a lot of credit at a big rate of interest, and you will have to constantly worry about repaying it. In the worst-case scenario, you might end up selling the house you bought.

Bad credit is difficult to deal with because once you have a few derogatory marks on your credit, it can take years to bring your score back up. A lot of the time with banks, you can't explain to them the reasoning behind the remarks, it is an automatic "no". This can be bey9ohnd frustrating for someone who has worked toward credit recovery for years but still has the shroud of past derogatory marks on their record. With accounts in collections, the best thing you can do is call and pay them off in full. If that isn't financially possible, pay back the creditors in regular monthly payments so the bank can see the effort you are putting into your credit. Get credit cards and don't spend them – only spend them if your intent is to go home and transfer money back onto them.

Exposure

When you wish to purchase property, you will be required to declare all your assets and everything else that you own. This means that you expose your financial holdings to the world around you. It can be a bad thing if you own a lot of money and you will have to declare it all. Even if you have a little money, you have to declare whatever that you own and give your creditor a clear picture of whatever you have in your possession. This can make some people uneasy, as their financial status will come under the scanner.

One of the important things to remember is that everyone has to go through this to get to where you are going. You are not the first person to have to expose themselves in this way, and you certainly won't be the last. Taking things like this to heart can really cause people to look negatively at the whole process when in reality, it's necessary. For example, say you were going to loan someone $150,000 because they told you they couldn't afford to purchase a home without a loan. Would you take their word for it and give them the money? Or would you check to make sure that they were telling the truth and really didn't have the money? What would it say about someone who lied about their income only to find out they have more than enough to pay for their home. Exposure has other intents besides checking finances. It says a lot about people's character if they lie about their income.

Illiquidity

Illiquidity refers to selling your property and the difficulties that you might face in doing so. If a worst-case scenario were to ever crop up, then you might have to do away with your property. But it is easier said than done and you might not have ready buyers for it. This can put you in a fix. So it is best to buy property in a good location so that you get ready buyers for it. You must also become a member of a union where buyers and sellers often meet to discuss issues.

This is one of the facets in which research prior to buying your home is imperative. You can't buy a home because you "like it". You need to look at the surrounding homes from the past few years that have gone up for sale and how quickly they sold; if they did at all. You also need to see how the home properties have either risen or fallen over the years as this will give you a good idea of what your home could be worth 10 years from now. Most importantly, look at the neighborhood in which you are buying. If you are purchasing in a nicer, more desirable neighborhood, then you are likely to have buyers a lot quicker than if you were attempting to sell way out in the country or in a more impoverished area.

Calamities

Unforeseen natural calamities are always a danger for your real estate investments. Imagine a tsunami striking and washing away your house or an earthquake creating a big crack in your house. All these can seriously damage your property and cause you to worry unnecessarily. Even if you have insurance, major damage to your property can never be fixed, and you will end up worrying about your investment. Although it is rare for such a calamity to occur, it is still a possibility and should be considered a disadvantage.

You can never know when disaster will strike – that's why they turn into disasters. If we all knew when hurricanes and tornadoes would hit, we would know when to leave and when to come back. We would have time to properly prepare our homes for the damage to come. Since we are unable to predict the Earths wrath, we are forced to keep calamities such as these in mind when purchasing a home. You can't predict when disasters will strike but you can prepare for them to the best of your ability by making sure your home and yard doesn't flood, there are no leakages in the roof, walls or windows and, the roof is up to date and sturdy. For areas that are more hurricane or heavy wind prone, hurricane shutters are a great investment.

Bad tenants

Dealing with bad tenants is always a major headache. They can completely ruin your property and make it unrecognizable. Even if you give your house to people who are disciplined, they might have young children who will ruin your walls and furniture. Keeping an eye on them constantly is not possible and you might have to move into a house close to your house for it. This is the number 1 reason why people don't wish to rent out their houses to others.

Like disasters, you never can predict when someone is going to be a "bad" tenant or not. Sometimes everything on paper looks great, even the first impression upon meeting the potential tenant. However, looks can be deceiving and what is on paper is the past, not the future. If you have a gut feeling upon meeting someone, follow it. There is a reason you are getting this feeling. Bad tenants can put you out of money for months when they don't pay rent, they damage the premises upon leaving and they force you to begin the eviction process. The time, money and energy involved in dealing with bad tenants can be enough to run a landlord out of the rental business altogether. Try and stay on the same page as your tenants. Respond to issues in the apartment immediately after they are reported and have the tenants sign a paper stating that you responded and what further action is going to be done or has been done. Cover your bases.

Foreign investors

Foreign investors will have a tough time investing in a foreign land. Expats and those wishing to settle down in a foreign country will have a lot of headaches when it comes to choosing and buying a property for themselves. They will have to pay more and they will get taxed both in the foreign country and their home country. So these laws make it difficult for foreigners to buy and sell properties.

Understandably so, some items such as homes are cheaper in the United States than they are in places like England and other parts of Europe. If it were easy for individuals to own real estate from other countries, it would be a mad house trying to sort through the paperwork overseas and attempt to communicate with a landlord that you have never seen. People in America tend to be weary when they don't meet an individual they are renting from because there are so many opportunities for scams that the risk just doesn't outweigh the benefits.

These form the disadvantages of investing in real estate. But don't worry, these should not stop you from making your investment and should only be seen as cautionary information to safeguard your investments.

Chapter 4: Tips for Beginners

As beginners, you will need quite a lot of help with hunting and buying your properties. In this chapter, we will look at some tips for beginners that will help you make the right choice for yourself.

Do your reading

The first thing to do is read extensively. This means that you immerse yourself into the know how of property buying and renting. You have to find all the best sources to gain information on the topic. The Internet is a good source no doubt, but you cannot trust everything that you read on it. So be selective and choose information that is good for you as a beginner and will provide you proper guidance through your property, and real estate, buying process.

Learn about the process of purchasing a home, what your rights as a purchaser are, where you can cut corners financially to save money; everything. You want to go into the home buying process with as much knowledge as you can gain so you are at less risk of being taken advantage of (which usually won't happen, but you never know) and will also give you a sense of confidence and empowerment as you understand the process while it unfolds. The more you read, the better. Visit websites for first time home buyers where they talk about struggles they had and things they may have missed before moving in. Sometimes, people miss key things such as a home inspection prior to signing papers because they are too caught up and distracted by everything else. Read everything, make a list and stick to it.

No expertise required

Many people feel overwhelmed at the presence of a plethora of information. This can seem quite daunting, and the person might not be able to separate the right from the wrong. But in any case, it is not important for you to be an expert on the subject and you can make the right choice for yourself just by doing a little reading on the subject. Of course having an expert opinion will make things easier for you, but it is not an absolute necessity. You can have just 1/3rd the knowledge of a real estate agent and yet make a good choice for yourself.

What is great about real estate investing is it is really easy to find information on and required no initial background knowledge or education to get started in the field. You can simply read an article or pick up a book to begin your real estate investing adventure. There is so much knowledge about the "do's" and "don'ts" when getting into the real estate investing market that it really does help you to prepare for all scenarios. You can take the book knowledge and apply it to the contextual knowledge so you can be better prepared for all potential scenarios. You want to know what everything means before you sign it as well as what it means if the contract is not carried out or followed.

Understand language

When it comes to property buying, you have to understand the basic language that is used. This can be short forms for the dimensions of a place or some lingo or code words for a particular type of property etc. When you know these words, you will have the chance to converse freely with the agent and also thoroughly understand what they are speaking about. Your chances of being fooled or taken for a ride will lessen, and you will have the chance to make the right choice for yourself.

Understanding real estate language is trying to understand medical terminology without ever setting foot in a medical setting. It can be daunting and confusing, while also making you feel stupid and slightly concerned about what is being talked about. Before heading in to speak with a real estate agent or making a phone call, make sure you know the lingo and all the potential facets about the home buying process that you both may go over. Knowing what to expect and why, while also knowing what it is the agent is talking about, can create a much less stressful and significantly more productive environment for both of you.

Save up

One important thing that a beginner must do is start saving up money for a property investment. You will have to save money wherever possible in order to be prepared to take a loan or avail credit and pay it all back within a short period of time. Borrowing money for a long time is not a good choice at all, and you must try your best to pay as little interest on your borrowing as possible. That will make your property buying experience a smooth, and happy, journey.

Saving money should be started as soon as the slightest inkling of investment is entertained. Once you begin to toss around the idea of investments, you are going to need money to invest. Saving can not only allow you to make the investments that you desire to make but also gives you a buffer or emergency fund in case your investments plummet or go sour. You don't want to purchase a home with only enough saved to pay the down payment and buyer/seller fees. You want to have several month's mortgage payment saved in case something happens with the home or if one of you is injured for whatever reason and is out of work. Savings, save lives. Figuratively and literally.

Know your numbers

While buying property, it is important for you to understand basic math and also some advanced calculations. Of course, it will not be extremely tough like college math, but you will have to be adept at making quick calculations. This will ensure that you are doing all the right calculations at the right time and know if you are paying the right amount or the wrong. If you are not good at calculating fast enough, then you must carry a calculator with you when you head out to find yourself a property.

You can practice at home with a pen and paper to sort of, map it out in your brain or you3.0 can stick with the calculator as previously mentioned. Most of the time, numbers can be calculated quickly via computer when working with a real estate agent but if you are out hunting on your own and trying to get a good idea of pricing, taxes, percentages, etc. then you will need to be able to calculate quickly and efficiently while also staying focused. If you need help with numbers such as tax percentages, carry a binder with you with different types of resources and tax percentages per state. This will make it much easier for you to buy and rent homes.

Have a plan

The golden rule for all new property investors is to have a plan of action. This means having a set plan to follow that will carve the way ahead. If you don't plan it out, then you will find it difficult to go about the process and get confused. Imagine going to a new city without a map – you are bound to get lost. So it is important for you to choose a plan of action and go about it in an organized manner. This plan need not be an elaborate one. You can list it out stepwise and mention everything including financing, hunting, buying, signing, renovating and renting. Each of these steps should further be divided into further steps.

Having a plan is imperative so that you can stick to your financial budget and know your course of action. Having a plan and writing one out may feel redundant, especially if this isn't your first time buying a real estate property, however, it needs to be incorporated each and every time you decide to purchase a property because without a plan you are at risk of straying from the plan. When you don't have guidelines to follow, you don't have any organization.

Consult

Sometimes it is important to consult an expert while buying a house or property. You will have to ask and know about several small things and understand what it means to buy a house in a particular locality. This expert can be a property expert or someone you know has made many investments made. Jot down everything that you wish to know about property buying and have your queries answered one by one. Once you have all your questions answered, you can go through it and understand it thoroughly.

Consultations can be a great way to learn more about the real estate investment industry. It may be difficult to admit that a consultation would be a good idea because some people like to do everything on their own as opposed to asking for help however consultations are usually free and can give you great insight into the industry that may not be available online. A lot of the time, the real estate agent that you are consulting with may be in the business a long time so the vast amount of experience can be incredibly beneficial. Consultations are also great, as stated previously, to answer any questions to may have about the industry and what may possibly arise.

Start small

One piece of advice for all beginners is to start small. There is no point in starting big as you will get confused and not know how to handle your finances. You might end up making unnecessary errors and lose out on money. So it is important for you to start small and look for a small house or an apartment that does not require a large investment. Look online to find an ideal place. If you like a small place, then inspect it personally and see if you like the neighborhood. Once you buy a small house, you will develop the confidence to buy a bigger property and make better investments.

As they say, "just take one bite at a time." Don't bite off more than you can chew, stick to one thing at a time and you will slowly, one by one, complete your real estate investment purchase. As with anything that requires a vast amount of information intake, paperwork and navigation, not keeping your cool and taking one small step at a time is incredibly important in keeping organized and on track. Becoming overwhelmed is easy to do so whenever the stress builds up, walk away to avoid becoming overwhelmed and possibly miss stepping.

Keep track

Remember to always keep track of everything that you have and all the investments that you make. Carry a small journal with you everywhere that you go and jot everything down. When you buy a property, you will be so busy and engrossed in whatever you are doing that you will forget about many small things. To help remember it better, you will have to carry the journal or even a digital diary that will allow you to jot down all the various points. You must refer back to it every now and then to refresh your memory and remember things better.

Writing everything down is a great practice. Even better than writing it down, type it out at the end of the day and print it. Place it in a folder with the date. This is good especially if it is your first real estate purchase because it can show you a paper trail and keep a record of the process you went through your first time. You can look back on the process and reference it in the future, or if anything comes up that may seem odd or incorrect, you can use your paper trail or notes to reference and make sure you are on track.

Sell, buy

If you already have a house, like an ancestral house, then you must know how to sell the previous one and buy a new one. It can seem quite daunting but something that needs to be done at any cost, especially if you dislike your old house. It is important to find the right price for your existing house and buy a new one that costs lesser than what you sold your old house for. This will ensure that you are left with some money that can be directed towards renovating the new house.

In order to find out the right price for your home, check the neighborhood statistics for what the homes are going for and what they have previously sold for. You can also have your home appraised once or twice to get a good idea of what your home may be worth. It is a good idea to start high and lower it as you go. The higher you start, the more room for negotiating that you have. When picking a new house to purchase, while also making sure it is cheaper than your current home, you need to also make sure the amount of renovations that need to be done don't exceed the amount of profit you have left over, or you will have no breathing room or financial flexibility.

You are halfway done!

Congratulations on making it to the halfway point of the journey. Many try and give up long before even getting to this point, so you are to be congratulated on this. You have shown that you are serious about getting better every day. I am also serious about improving my life, and helping others get better along the way. To do this I need your feedback. Click on the link below and take a moment to let me know how this book has helped you. If you feel there is something missing or something you would like to see differently, I would love to know about it. I want to ensure that as you and I improve, this book continues to improve as well. Thank you for taking the time to ensure that we are all getting the most from each other.

Chapter 5: Types Of Real Estate Properties

There are many types of real estate properties that you can choose from and buy for yourself. In this chapter, we will look at the different types, and what each one is capable of providing you with.

Residential real estate properties

Residential real estate properties, as the name suggests, incorporates houses, vacation homes, condos, villas, etc. These are probably the most common type of real estate investments that people make.

When you buy a house or a flat, you have the choice to stay there yourself or rent or lease it out. If you occupy it yourself, then you will not have any monetary advantage but will have a sense of pride and belonging. But if you rent or lease it out then you will have a monetary advantage and can make money out of your investment. This is only possible if you already have a place to stay at.

Multi-family residential property is a good choice for you as you can rent out your house to someone and receive a consistent income. You can buy a plot and construct 5 or 6 houses and rent all of them out so that even if one or two houses remain vacant, the others will help you earn an income.

These are great properties to own but can be difficult do maintenance on all the properties, especially if they are located long distances from one another. With multiple homes, it is a good idea to employ a reliable handyman to do the work for you so you can spend your time doing other jobs such as scouting for new homes or working on your financial portfolio. There are a lot of homes available for purchase and sometimes you can find great homes through foreclosure websites or auctions. It is important to look around at all your options so you don't spend more money than you have to for your real estate investment property.

Some other great properties are large residential buildings such as apartment complexes or duplexes. A lot of the time, older duplexes can be purchased for a decent amount of money and can be remodeled and rented out for a large profit. These large complexes bring in a large amount of profit as due to this, it is easy to expand. However, with these types of buildings you need to also offer services such as a pool, gym, laundry facilities, etc. Also, when one apartment is in trouble, (fire, flood, etc.) it puts the rest of the homes at risk so the issues need to be dealt with promptly.

The taxation and maintenance costs will have to be decided upon, and either you or your tenant will have to pay it.

Commercial real estate properties

Commercial real estate properties include office buildings, buildings lent to commercial establishments, etc. All these are only affordable to those who have a big investment capacity. Commercial real estate properties are tough to start off with, and you will have to own a residential property first to understand what it takes to invest in such properties.

Once you buy a building, you must look for ideal tenants. Your tenants will be business houses looking for an office space. You can charge them rent, but the general rule for commercial establishments is to pay the lease. This lease will help you repay your debts with ease.

These buildings are often more enjoyable to rent because your tenants are usually with you for several years to decades. Once you have a tenant with a great and growing business, it will bring more business to the other businesses and in turn, keep you tenants and their businesses busy and happy. These buildings, as stated before, are significantly easier to maintain because most businesses take care of their own problems every day such as vacuuming, window cleaning, sweeping the outside of the store, sanitizing the inside, etc. Any damage they do to the interior of the building would reflect badly on their business so, for the most part, business owners can be the best types of tenants.

The maintenance for office buildings is less as compared to residential investments. This is because offices are generally maintained by maintenance staff, and any damage will be charged to the tenant. So you can safeguard your property and have a good time reeling in profits.

Industrial real estate properties

Industrial real estate investments are those that are directed towards buying storage units, garages, car washes, industrial establishments, etc. here, you have the choice to rent out a fully equipped station or simply give away some industrial space. It will depend on the investment that you have made towards the property.

Money needed for this type of investment is much lesser as compared to the previous category. Here, you will need lesser money owing to the size of the property, and your average cost will work out to be cheaper.

You also may need more permits for this location than other locations. For example, a car washing business will produce a lot of waste that could potentially flow into the drains and cause issues with the sanitation systems and water quality. Due to this, certain areas may not allow certain types of businesses. You would be a lot less likely to legally purchase an industrial real estate place located adjacent to the ocean and use it as a recycling or waste disposal company or a car wash because of the high risk of run off and pollution into the ocean. This goes for industrial businesses that may use heav y machinery and could pose a threat to pedestrians within close range; you wouldn't be able to purchase a lot and legally use it for a business that could potentially harm bystanders or pedestrians. There is a lot to keep in mind when looking for industrial real estate locations so it is important to do even more research on potential properties than other types of investments.

However, there will be a million small things to look into while buying an establishment of this sort. You will have to look into the dimensions of the space, the location, the connectivity, the neighborhood, etc. If the location is bad, then you will have to look for a better one, as you don't want to get into trouble later.

Retail real estate properties

Retail real estate properties are those that include the likes of shops, malls, storefronts, etc. You can buy an entire mall and rent it out or just a single shop in it. This is an advanced investment, and you will need quite a substantial amount to invest in it.

Again, you will have to look for a lot of things like the location, the size, the reach, the connectivity, the ambience, the neighborhood, etc. Once you like the place, you will have to sign many forms before you can own the place.

When you have an entire mall to lend, you must find a good anchor for yourself. Anchors are big retailers that will help you draw in the crowds. For example a store like Target, which will ensure that people visit your mall, and help keep it busy. This is a good investment choice for you, as the returns you will earn from it will be quite substantial and stable.

Retail establishments are also great investments, especially when, as stated earlier, they are purchased in their entirety (such as a strip mall or mall type setting). With strip malls, you can gauge your tenants based on the types of businesses that are already there so you don't double up businesses and create negativity and drop sales of other businesses. For example, you wouldn't rent out two different spaces to coffee shops in the same strip mall. You also wouldn't open two different discount shoe stores either. You can see what stores are popular and reach out to potential businesses looking to expand, or that may be a great addition to the traffic at your retail real estate investment.

Mixed properties

Mixed properties are those that combine the various different categories into one building or location.

So you have an office building on one end, a retail mall on the other and a residential complex in between. Of course, this will end up being a very costly affair, but you will have the chance to make up for all your expenses in no time. But you will have to approach a bank or a creditor to finance your project and show proof that you are capable of owning something so big.

There are a bunch of options here because you have such a wide range of available business ventures for potential tenants. You give people the option of having an office space while also giving an option for restaurants and retail stores to populate the mall as well. For example, a real estate firm or law firm may populate on end of the strip mall and on the other end there is a coffee shop and a hair salon. Both of these businesses will benefit interdependently off one another by networking and getting to know each other. Other businesses will also make their way into the premises and as they do, more networking and bonds will be created. These sorts of mixed establishments are great because different businesses and utilize the services of others; law firm attends the coffee shop for lunch and morning coffee and the coffee shop uses the law firm for their contracts, legal contracts and consultations.

Here too, you will have to carefully choose a location, as there will be several things to consider. The diversification will ensure that you have a consistent stream of money coming your way and at no time will your incomes cease.

Rent to own

Renting to own is another great way to obtain property but it can take a long time to actually, legally own the property. With rent to own, you are essentially paying off someone else's mortgage because they don't what the home anymore, with the agreement that you will own the home once the mortgage is paid off in full. You have to be careful with rent to own properties and read the contract fully because many people have been scammed once the mortgage is paid off; meaning, the original home owners put a loop hole in the contract so they could get the home back once it was paid off. It is hard to believe, ethically, that people would do that but it has happened before and it will happen again.

With rent to own properties, you don't have to come up with a large down payment like you would if you were taking out a large loan on your own and you also don't have to worry about qualifying for a good interest rate or putting yourself in a massive amount of debt by obtaining a mortgage. In some cases, you can rent out your "rent to own home" as well but you have to make sure there is nothing in your contract with the original home owners that states you can't do so.

Rent to own is a great option for someone who is still working on their credit but desires to be a homeowner and can't qualify for their own home loan. As I stated before, I can't stress enough the importance of making sure the contract is sound, having a lawyer of your own look over it and then looking it over again before you sign it.

Foreign properties

Foreign properties refer to buying properties, or real estate, in a foreign country. It's a great option for expats to buy a house in their home country and one in their adopted country. It will be a herculean task but nothing that is impossible. There will be a hundred things to look into like the taxation policy, the price offered to foreigners, any surcharges, certificates, legal documents etc. But all of it will pay off in the end if you make the right choice for yourself.

The challenges with foreign properties are the inability to always be there when something on or in the property goes wrong. You have to hire a reliable handyman to take care of the property to avoid work orders going unfixed. It can also be difficult to find tenants because a lot of people are weary of working with landlords or tenants across the country because of the high risk for fraudulent activity. Though not nearly as prevalent as it used to be due to public awareness of the issue, fraudulent activity is most common with foreign landlords or people "claiming" to be landlords for certain properties.

Miscellaneous

Apart from the types of real estate choices mentioned above, there are a few more miscellaneous ones and they are as follows.

Construction

It is always a good idea to buy a plot of land and construct your own house. What this will do is, help you save a lot of money. You will only have to pay a minimum for the construction materials and avail discount for buying it in bulk. Labor charges can also be reduced. Moreover, you will have the chance to plan the entire project from scratch and incorporate design elements that will suit your taste. Many people don't like what they buy and end up further hating what they do to the house. All this can be avoided by buying a piece of land in a nice locality and building your own house. If a house already exists then you can partially renovate it or raze it to the ground and start afresh.

Sometimes, you can get a home for an incredibly cheap price and then bulldoze it once the home is purchased. Then, you can build the home you desire on the plot of land or keep the land and sell it when it appreciates in value over time. Land can be incredibly expensive but as long as you shop around, specifically for foreclosed homes and short sales, you can obtain a home and land for an incredibly great value and essentially start from scratch. It may seem daunting to tear down a home to reconstruct but the process is simple if the same, careful steps are followed just like navigating the home buying process.

Container homes

The newest property fetish to hit the real estate market is container homes. Container homes are made out of tin containers that are abandoned by cargo companies. These are picked up and refurbished by retail companies, who sell them to you at discounted prices. All you have to do is choose an ideal piece of land and stack these containers one above the other. You can have separate containers come together to form an ideal home. The possibilities are endless and you can decorate them however you like.

Container homes are the latest craze, similar to the tiny, mobile home units. People are constantly looking for cheaper, DIY ways to obtain homes without having to navigate the stressful and confusing real estate world. Buying your own land and placing shipping containers on it may require permits of some sort but for the most part, you are on your own and people like it that way. In a world dictated by laws, regulations and things you can and can't do, being able to create your own home by purchasing a shipping container for as cheap as $800 and as high as $3,000 seems incredibly enticing for someone who is passionate about DIY home projects and handy work.

Recreational properties

Recreational properties are those that you buy and use for recreational purposes. These are generally seen as vacation homes, but you can make it your full time home if you wish to. You can choose a serene location like between the hills or in the middle of the forest. If a ready-made home is not available, then you can buy a plot of land and build a house over it. You can also rent or lease it out to people or treat it as a commercial vacation stay home. The returns you earn from this kind of investment can be quite high!

A lot of the time, these types of properties are known as timeshares or vacation rentals. Either, or – though both are quite different. With vacation homes, you usually have one dwelling that is owned by you that you rent out seasonally to snow birds or short stays like weekend getaways or people coming into town for a week. With this being said, vacation homes can be beneficial by allowing you, the owner, to vacation there while not having to pay a price (because you own it) and then continuing to rent it out recreationally once you are done vacationing there.

With timeshares, buildings, cabins, homes, etc. are purchased for an amount of time each year. For example, the Adams family purchased the time share for the entire month of January, and the Johnson family purchased the same time share for the last two weeks in January. You are essentially renting out the home to a bunch of different people, but they are sharing the property by purchasing a time to come and always owning that time slot until their contract or lease expires.

These form the various types of properties that you can buy and rent or lease if you like. It is possible for you to own all of these if you take the right steps. But it will take a long time and patience will pay off. There is also the option of buying a house today, living in it for 5 years and then buying another one and moving in without paying any tax on it. But for that, you will have to be ready to move out of a place easily without getting too attached to the place.

Chapter 6: Mistakes To Avoid While Real Estate Investing

When it comes to real estate investing, you have to avoid certain mistakes that can cause your investment to go bad. In this chapter, we look at these mistakes in detail and help you get on the right track.

Paying too much

One thing to remember is to never over pay for a property. After all, it is your hard earned money that you will be investing in the property. So it is important that you not end up over paying and pay just the right amount for your property. If you think the seller is charging you too much, then ask them to reduce the price and haggle until the two of reach a price that is closer to what you wish to pay. But if you do over pay, then think of it as a learning curve and don't repeat the same mistake again.

One of the ways to keep from overpaying is to make sure you do your research on the surrounding properties around the one you are looking at purchasing. If the properties around you are all worth $250,000, and the only you are looking at is priced at $325,000, you have the ability to do a large amount of negotiating with the seller. You can also ask how much to home was appraised for and ask for the paperwork so you can make sure the home is worth what the seller is selling it for. Before purchasing, you also need to calculate how much your mortgage payment is going to be and how much you can charge for rent.

Looking without money

Many people start to hunt for a property without having proper financial backing. This is the wrong thing to do, as you won't have a budget to work with. You will end up over paying for something and not know how your budget was over shot. In fact, you might get in to the deal and not have any money to pay to the seller. That can get you into a lot of trouble. So it is important for you to not start looking for properties without having the proper financial backing and only start after you have money in your account.

Mentally, looking without money can take a toll on you and cause you to make irresponsible decisions out of a desire to have a financial blanket. It can be frustrating not being able to look at properties because of the lack of finance's but use this frustration as motivation to save, work on your credit and do the research involved to make smart decisions. Think of the lack of finances as an opportunity to educate yourself more than individuals who already have the finances and as a result, make better and smarter decisions leading to a better, passive income. However, you can also look for potential properties that may soon come available within the time frame of your financial savings.

Not doing research

Never refrain from doing your homework before buying a property. It is vital for you to conduct your research before buying a property of your choice. If you feel lazy, then you will end up with a lousy house. So don't turn away from hard work and put in as much as you can. Sit down for an hour every day and conduct a simple research. You will understand how helpful it is to use the knowledge that you gain out of your daily research.

This is one of the most important things to remember to not do... not research. Without research, you won't be able to successfully participate in the real estate investing market because you won't know which steps to take and when. Doing your research is imperative to making the right decisions without making mistakes because mistakes in the real estate business could lead to bankruptcy and financial ruin. Dealing with real estate should only be done after extensive research is done and if it isn't, help from either a real estate firm or a friend or family member who is familiar with the real estate process.

Not liking property

Never buy a property that you do not like. It is a big mistake to buy a house that is not to your liking. You will not be happy with your investment and it will turn into a headache for you. You will want to invest in something else that you like and get rid of your property at the earliest. So before you sign on the dotted line, make sure you thoroughly inspect the property and buy it only if you like it. If you don't, then don't worry, there will be a million other options available out there that you can buy for yourself and lead a happy life.

Depending on the reason you don't like the property, there may or may not be a way to fix the property. If the problem is constant repairs due to the old age of the property, you can have an inspection to see if the foundation is solid and if it is, you can completely remodel the home to your liking. The same goes for cosmetic dislike. If you have the finances, you can remodel the home to your liking but keep in mind your tastes may not be the same as other individuals. When decorating, choose neutral colors and neutral décor. As far as foundation issues and irreparable damage is concerned, you may have no other choice than to tear the property down and start from scratch. It is important to like a property before you buy it – remember this and you won't have to deal with this in the future.

Assuming things

Never assume things, especially when it comes to the price of the house. You have to know everything that there is to about an investment and have the exact details about it. If you assume things, then you will end up feeling disappointed with your investment. So have everything clearly mapped out and don't assume anything. You will make a real estate investment just once in your life so make sure you do all the right things from the get go.

Never assume things, everything needs to be done with facts, knowledge and research. When you assume things, you are setting yourself up for failure. When you go to school and take a test, you can't assume that the answers you are choosing are right, you need to know.

Doing everything by yourself

It is understood that you will have a lot of excitement while buying your first house. But that does not mean you do everything by yourself. You have to take care of a million things, and it will not be possible for you to do everything single handedly. Employ a friend or a sibling or someone who can lend you a helping hand in hunting and finalizing a house. Just make sure the other person is just as interested as you are in the project and don't coerce anyone to help you.

Some people prefer to do everything by themselves. This isn't a good idea when it involves something as complicating and stressful as real estate because even if you know how to do everything, you still need someone to talk to and help you through the difficult times. As tempting as doing things by yourself can be, you still need to have a support system.

Miscalculating

The worst thing you could end up doing is miscalculating. It is very important for you to get your math correct and know exactly how much you need to pay your creditors. Sit down with a friend who has expert knowledge on the subject and get them to help you with the math. It is important for you to know exactly how much you must pay the seller, how much you owe the bank and the interest being charged. Never over pay the interest and check your bank statement regularly to see if any erroneous entries have been made.

Miscalculating can be an easy thing to do, but you need to ensure that miscalculating doesn't happen. In order to make sure your numbers are correct, you can employ the services of an accountant or a professional in the area of real estate finances to ensure that your numbers are correct, and there are no miscalculations. Miscalculating is even easier to do when there is a large amount of numbers and paperwork that you are dealing with. You need to make sure you are thorough.

Time frame

Many people do not take into consideration the time that it will take for them to find a house, buy it, renovate it and then rent it. In all of this, renting it out will take the maximum time and until such time, the owner must pay the maintenance, the taxes, etc. so all of it should be taken into consideration when setting a particular time frame for a property investment.

With that being said, you don't want to rush the time frame because you are impatient. Impatience can get you into trouble. You need to make sure you understand how long the process can take, and you need to be willing to ride it out. Granted, it is nice when things happen faster, but there is a reason for the time frame. Trying to push things faster than the time frame could cause errors in paperwork and could be deceiving whereas moving things slower than normal could pose a problem for both you and the seller since you both are in need to relocation.

One exit strategy

When you buy a house, don't have only one exit strategy from the deal. You never know when a deal might go bad, even if it is a dream project. You cannot have any one-exit strategy alone and must think of two or three different strategies. This will ensure that you do not get stuck and can exit from a bad deal easily.

Having one exit strategy can be a terrible idea. You need to have at least three exit strategies in case things don't go as planned – which happens quite often. Do your exit strategy along these lines "If this doesn't happen, then we will do this and if that doesn't happen, we will do this. If all of those things can't happen then this is the plan". This will save you if your first two plans don't work out for whatever reason. If you are unsure about how to formulate more than one plan out, speak with a lawyer or a real estate agent that you are on good terms with. Real estate agents are on the side of the seller for the most part, but if you can find an unbiased agent to speak with or consult, this would be your best bet for formulating exit strategies.

Trusting agents

It is extremely important for you to understand that estate agents are always only there to help the sellers and not the buyers. If you think the agent will help you buy a good property, then you are wrong. The agent is employed by the seller and not the buyer so don't blindly trust anything that the agent says to you and do your own research before making the deal final.

If you know the agent personally (friend or family member) then you may be more apt to trust them because you know they have your best interest and the sellers best interest in mind. However, for the most part, trusting insurance agents can be risky. They are being paid by the seller and once the house sells, they get a percentage. With this being said, you are more likely to work more favorably towards someone who is paying you based on selling their home than you are towards someone who may or may not purchase the home. Although you probably won't have to deal with a lawyer that is crooked or untrustworthy, however they do exist and you need to be prepared if you have to deal with one.

These form the various mistakes you must avoid while buying a real estate property for yourself.

Chapter 7: Real Estate Finance Sources

When it comes to financing your project, you will require a certain sum of money to start off with. This money can be your personal money, or borrowed from a relative. This money will be paid in advance to the seller. Remember, a bank or other such financial institution will only pay you 80% of the amount, and the rest should be your money.

In this chapter, we will look at the various sources of finance that you can approach to fund your real estate investment.

Bank loans

The first and most popular form of finance are bank loans. Any bank, government or commercial, will be ready to finance your project, provided you are the right candidate for it. There are more than 20,000 banks in America, and you can choose anyone to fund your investment. The bank will give you many options, and you have to choose the one that suits your requirements. The basic idea is to avail a loan with a lower rate of interest and try and repay it at the earliest possible time. If you know a friend or someone who works at the bank then you can ask them to help you expedite your process.

Some bank loans can be difficult to qualify for, even if you know someone at the bank. There are a lot of different ways to go about obtaining a bank loan, however, most of the time you need good credit in order to qualify for one with a good, affordable interest rate.

Home equity line of credit

Home equity line of credit (HELOC) is a way to afford to purchase a home if you can't purchase it yourself. As defined by Consumer Finance, "A home equity line of credit is a form of revolving credit in which your home serves as collateral. Because a home often is a consumer's most valuable asset, many homeowners use home equity credit lines only for major items, such as education, home improvements, or medical bills, and choose not to use them for day-to-day expenses."

Lenders will take into account your ability to pay back the credit and what your interest rate will be. Using a home equity line of credit can help you get through difficult times in your life by using your home as collateral.

Raising capital to finance your home

Raising capital to finance your home can be done a multitude of different ways. Listed below are nearly all the ways in which one can raise capital to finance their home or property investments.

Credit unions

Credit unions are like cooperative societies for finance. Credit unions are formed by members who contribute money toward the society. This money is pooled in and maintained as a fund. If any member needs money, then they are given the money at a certain interest rate. This rate is always much lower than what commercial banks would charge. So you will end up getting the loan at a faster pace and at an interest rate that is much lower than what creditors or banks would charge you.

Credit unions are a great option for people who have less than desirable credit. They are also great for getting lower interest rates than what normal, commercial banks offer. They are great options for younger individuals who don't have an established credit history or who are recovering from derogatory marks on their credit, late payments, repossession, etc. If you know you are going to get a higher interest rate from a commercial bank; credit unions are the way to go.

Life insurance corporations

Life insurance corporations will also lend money to people looking for finance. When you buy a life insurance policy, you pay a certain sum towards it on a monthly basis. If you wish to avail finance for a project, then you can approach your insurance company and ask for a loan. They will give it to you provided you return the money back along with a certain interest. This interest depends on the company and differs from company to company. This is a great scheme as you will not have to pay a lot of interest and the money will ultimately come back to you itself.

It may be difficult to qualify for a loan from your life insurance company if you haven't been established with them for a long period of time. It may also be difficult if you haven't held down a steady source of reliable income or have a part time job. If you have life insurance through your employer, it may be a bit easier to get a loan. Again, this all depends on your company, your financial history and how likely you are to pay back the loan with interest, on time.

Mortgage brokers

Mortgage brokers are those middlemen who help borrower meet with a capital seller. So they will help you find someone who will finance your project and gets the project rolling. These brokers will not directly fund you and will only help you meet these creditors. For their services provided, they will charge you 1% of your total borrowings. This is not so bad considering you will find it tough to find a capital investor by yourself. These brokers are all the more necessary if you are trying to buy a house in a foreign land.

Mortgage brokers aren't used nearly as often as they used to be. However, they come in handy for different circumstances. It can be difficult to figure out what exactly you need to qualify for a loan or a line of credit to finance your home, and these mortgage brokers will help you. They can lay out a plan for you to follow and a set of guidelines that will build your credit and make you more likely to qualify for a decent line of credit. It may also be a great idea to use them as consultation services as well, as they can answer many questions you may have about mortgages and mortgage payments.

Finance companies

Financial companies provide you with mortgage assistance. They will help you out financially and charge you a rate of interest like a commercial bank would. Back in the day when banks did not exist, only finance companies operated. But as time passed their importance started to deplete. However, they are still in operation and will provide you a loan at a nominal rate, or a competing rate. But you can have your loan sanctioned faster and go ahead with your project.

Finance companies are ideal for people who are going through a difficult financial period or who aren't able to afford their initial mortgage payments due to miscalculation or loss of a job. They are rarely used due to the drop in loans being offered after the housing market crash, as stated previously. Although not the ideal situation, they can be beneficial to some individuals in times of crisis but should generally be avoided unless absolutely necessary because before you buy a home, you need to make sure you can afford the mortgage.

Pension funds

Pension funds are also a good scheme to choose for your projects. These funds will help you borrow money for your project and use it to pay the seller. Just like insurance company borrowings, you will have to repay the money that you borrow from your pension fund and make sure you also pay a certain rate of interest on it. Apart from helping you with the money, some of these funds will also own certain properties and can help you find the right one for yourself.

It is not recommended to use these funds due to the likelihood of taxes and fees on them. There is also a chance that your investment will go sour, and you will not only be out of important retirement funds, but you will also be out of current living money. Taking out pension funds is something that needs to be highly researched before taking part in. You don't want to mess up your future because you weren't thinking clearly in the present. Pension funds are made for retirement and to help you survive when you no longer have a job; using these funds could be bad news.

REITS

As we read in the first chapter, REITS are equity trusts that are bought and sold on the stock exchange. They derive their capital from interest earned on portfolios and loan placement fees. They will be happy to help you find your project and also finance it. Requoting REITS from Chapter 1 to avoid you needing to backtrack, "REIT stands for real estate investment trust and is a security that is traded on the stock exchange. It helps indirectly investing in real estate properties and allows you to own a property in a short period of time. When you buy a REIT, then you will be contributing towards buying a property that is traded in the exchange. These REITs are funded by the rents that they receive from these properties. You can buy them directly from a stock exchange or indirectly through a mutual fund. You can combine it with a dividend reinvestment plan.

In other words, real estate investing trusts are companies that own properties that produce income (income producing properties). Within these trusts (companies), they own a variety of different real estate that produces income either residentially or commercially and can range from hospitals to warehouses to hair salons. As long as the property generates incomes, it can be within the real estate investing trust. They are originally derived from mutual funds, and they allow you to generate income from purchasing stocks as opposed to the entire property. Real estate investment trusts can be formed or joined; forming one requires that your business meets strict financial and organizational standards, numbers and regulations to be considered eligible."

Foreign funds

These refer to funds that foreign nationals will provide to you. This is ideal for you if you wish to invest in retail, industrial or multifamily residential properties. Foreign funding is a good choice if you are unable to get funding in your own country through your local resources. Many foreigners are interested in investing in the US owing to the lucrative real estate market that the country provides which comes with the added bonus of a stable economy.

It is much more expensive for an American to look for real estate elsewhere because other real estate markets in foreign countries are a bit more difficult to penetrate for a variety of reasons. It is also difficult to sort out your taxes at the end of the year if you own property in different countries. You also have to deal with a reliable maintenance or hand man that can frequent your foreign properties whenever there is an issue. Although it is more expensive and risky dealing with foreign properties, the financial benefit can be much greater than owning properties in the United States. Depending on location, owning property in desirable spots throughout Europe can bring in significant amounts of money year- round because of tourism.

Just because the market is more difficult to break into doesn't mean you should shy away from it if it is something that you are incredibly passionate about. Especially if you enjoy traveling; having homes and real estate in different countries would make traveling cheaper.

Government schemes

There are many government schemes, which provide you with finance for your projects. These schemes are aimed at helping people have their own homes. These will participate in the secondary mortgage market and provide loans to those in need. These will be willing to finance even high-risk ventures and provide loans to a wide category of people including youngsters and older people. They will charge a rate of interest that is not as high as what regular banks would charge and are a great option to all those that don't earn a lot of money.

There are programs like "first time home buyers" or second time home buyers that can all but eliminate a down payment for purchasing real estate. In some cases, the down payment is waived. After a significant amount of time passes, people are eligible to buy another home with low or none existent down payments. There are other types of accounts you can hold with different banks or credit unions such as Roth IRA's or traditional Roth's. Having these accounts can allow you to take out up to $10,000 of your savings tax free for first time home buyer fees.

This is great because the money in a Roth IRA is not allowed to be touched' only under certain circumstances. If you have to withdraw money from your Roth account before it is eligible, you are likely to deal with a high degree of taxation and walk away with over a quarter of your savings missing. However, if you use the $10,000 for home buyer's fees, this is untaxed, and there are no penalties.

Individual investors

There will be many individual investors interested in lending you money. These investors will have a lot of money already and will be looking to invest it in a good place. They will be willing to lend it to you provided you return it to them with interest. They will also be interested in availing other benefits such as getting a house at a discounted rate or membership in a builders club, etc. You can find out if there is any such person in your vicinity and approach them for finance.

Relatives

As a last resort, you can try borrowing from relatives. Although finding a single financier can be difficult, you can try to get the maximum from a single rich relative. You can also pool in money from friends and family and buy your property. If you rent it out, then you will get enough money, which you can distribute, to every one on a monthly basis. But make sure that some of the investment is your own money so that you don't have to deal with repaying the sum for a long time.

These form the various sources of finance that you can approach for your real estate investments.

Places to Look for Real Estate

Depending on the type of real estate you are looking for (and depending on the amount of time and ability you have to travel to your properties) there are a multitude of ways to search for real estate properties.

Online

When it comes to looking for listings, the best place to start is the Internet. You can find ads for houses, villas, condos, apartments, rent properties, sale properties, lease properties, etc. There is no dearth of websites available online that showcase property ads. All you have to do is look for a site that puts out ads of houses in your locality and contact the broker or the owner of the property. You can then personally inspect the property and talk terms with the owner. You must make sure you have been shown the right pictures of the property and have not been fooled. Once you are satisfied with everything, you can go ahead with the deal.

Online is a fantastic tool that at one time, wasn't available. Once it originally came about, the real estate online market was utilized nearly as much as it is now. There are many sites with which listings of all types can be found for free. There are also different foreclosure sites that sometimes require you to pay a one-time fee to be a part of, but you can usually find what you are looking for within a few months. Online can be both a blessing and a curse, as it is easy to pose as someone else online. There were several scams recently of people who were looking at homes to rent and spoke with someone they believed was the landlord of the property, they paid the deposit and move-in fees and went to move in, only to find there was a family already living there.

Turns out, the fraudulent landlord took photos from the property when it first came up for rent (or posted fake photos of the inside of a different home) and claimed he was the landlord. There is not much regulation when it comes to posting real estate on open online areas, so doing your research and meeting with the landlord in person to see the home before moving in is crucial.

Classifieds

Newspaper and magazine classifieds is a good place to look for ads. Remember that the best property ads will always be hidden and hard to find. They will not be publicized too much, and the owners will take the traditional approach. So buy yourself a local classifieds magazine or newspaper and go through it every now and then. Call up the owner and fix an appointment. Once you inspect the house personally, you can go ahead with the deal. But it is important to not rush into anything and take it slow.

Classifieds are rarely looked at anymore for rentals and sales because of the vast online market now available. This means that the classifieds are a perfect place to look because there isn't nearly as much competition as there used to be. What is interesting about the classified ads is it is one of the last, traditional ways of home searching other than driving around the neighborhood you want to live in and calling to speak with an agent. It is incredible how many people look past the classifieds when searching for homes for sale, missing so many opportunities.

Clubs / Unions

Becoming a member of a club or a union is a good idea. You will have the chance to interact with other buyers and more importantly, sellers. You will know what property is for sale where and at what price. You will have the opportunity to access a large variety and then choose the best one for yourself. Most of these builder clubs and associations will charge you a fee, but it will not be too high. You can continue being a member to avail constant updates on properties and their prices.

Agents

Although agents have earned a bad name for themselves owing to their tendency of tipping towards the sellers, there can be good agents available in your locality. They might charge you quite a bit, but they will have better access to all the best properties in the area. They will also help you avail financial assistance, as they will have contacts with a lot of creditors. So don't be afraid to contact a real estate agent, but don't make it your first option.

You shouldn't write off agents altogether after one bad experience, as a lot of the time, they will be more than willing to help you search for properties. Believe it or not, agents are a lot more responsive to your needs if you, the buyer, comes to them first willingly without being forced to work with one another through the seller. When agents are working with you, they are getting a percentage of your potential sale, so working with you to find the perfect home benefits them as well, which is why agents shouldn't be completely written off. Without agents, the real estate market would be significantly more frustrating and confusing than it already is, and there would probably be a lot more scamming and withholding of information unethically.

These form the different places where you can avail real estate listings. You might not hit jackpot immediately, but if you keep looking, then you might get the house of your dreams.

Key Highlights

The very first thing to understand about the real estate market is-how it operates. You must understand that there will be buyers and there will be sellers. You, as a buyer, must know who the sellers are and what they are offing to you. If you like the house and the price, then it is pretty straightforward. But if you like the house but not the price, then you must haggle and make sure you get the house at the right price.

The Internet is a great source to find houses and you can look up listings. But it is essential for you to insist on seeing the actual and real pictures of the house or property before deciding to buy it. Before buying, it is important for you to shortlist at least two houses and compare the two for prices, location and amenities. Once you make the choice, you can go ahead with the deal. But remember to never rush into anything and take your own time with it.

Real estate investments are a great choice for both beginners and those who already have a few investments made. The advantages to owning a property run into the hundreds and that is not an exaggeration. It can be pitted against all other firms of investments such as stock market investments, and you will realize that property investments are safe bets. They are also lucrative options and will ensure that your money is out to good use.

Apart from advantages, there are also certain disadvantages to look into. These need to be considered to understand that not everything in life will come with guarantees. You have to be prepared for the worst just as you would be prepared for the best. The disadvantages mentioned in this book are basic, and these are enough for you to know and understand to safeguard your investments.

There are different types of investments that you can make, and each one was explained in this book. It is highly possible for you to make more than one big investment but patience and diligence are key. You cannot decide today and buy a property tomorrow. You must conduct thorough research and decide upon a project that suits your needs. It is essential to avoid making the mistakes that can cause you to have a bad deal.

You can raise capital for your investment in any way you prefer. We looked at the different ways in which you can finance your project. You can choose any one of these methods and raise capital for your real estate investment. The degree of risk attached with each varies from source to source, and you must decide on the best one for yourself. The basic idea is to avail the credit at the lowest possible rate and not pay any penny extra.

Conclusion

I thank you once again for choosing this book and hope you enjoyed reading it.

The main aim of this book was to educate you on the topic of real estate investments, and how easy it is for you to buy and sell houses in the US.

This book is not all encompassing, but merely a detailed summary of different ways to purchase a home, steps to take before and after, where you can look for homes, dealing with real estate agents, navigating the home buying process and much, much more. This book is filled with the invaluable knowledge of the real estate investment market that you won't find anywhere else.

Once you make the choice to buy a property, all you have to do is follow a few basic steps, and you will have your own property in no time.

But you will have to do everything intelligently, and make sure that you walk away with the better deal.

Research, research and more research. This is one of the most important steps to ensure your real estate endeavor goes as smoothly and stress-free as possible. You can never know too much and the more you learn, the more prepared you will be in the long run when you begin to work with the seller and the realtor. You will also be able to tell if and when people are lying as well as pinpoint what steps need to be taken next.

Sticking to your budget, your timeline, and your plan are important as well. Don't forget to map out your steps and make sure everything is followed in a certain order and that no step is forgotten. Make a checklist if you have to and check it off as you go. Being prepared is not only a stress reliever for you, but also for the people you are working with because you are organized. People can't stand to make life decisions such as buying a home, with someone who has no idea what they are doing.

Approach all your deals and meetings with confidence, even if you are nervous. Being visibly nervous will only heighten the risk of being taken advantage of. If you are confident and knowledgeable about the system and how it works, then you won't have to worry about people, agents and sellers trying to pull one over on you.

Don't fall prey to any scams and remain as alert, and diligent, as possible while purchasing a property. Once you garner the confidence to buy a house, you will look for bigger and better investments.

Thanks again for choosing this book, I hope that you were able to gain valuable real estate investment knowledge that will guide you through the process of investing confidently. I hope that if you enjoyed the book, and you would recommend it to friends and family as well, giving you all a leg up in the real estate investment world. I wish you luck with all your real estate endeavors and hope you make the right choice for yourself. Remember, knowledge is power. Know you're your stuff and the rest will come easy.

All the best!

Free membership into the Mastermind Self Development Group!

For a limited time, you can join the Mastermind Self Development Group for free! You will receive videos and articles from top authorities in self development as well as a special group only offers on new books and training programs. There will also be a monthly member only draw that gives you a chance to win any book from your Kindle wish list!

If you sign up through this link http://www.mastermindselfdevelopment.com/specialreport you will also get a special free report on the Wheel of Life. This report will give you a visual look at your current life and then take you through a series of exercises that will help you plan what your perfect life looks like. The workbook does not end there; we then take you through a process to help you plan how to achieve that perfect life. The process is very powerful and has the potential to change your life forever. Join the group now and start to change your life! http://www.mastermindselfdevelopment.com/specialreport

CPSIA information can be obtained
at www.ICGtesting.com
Printed in the USA
LVHW051818150223
739590LV00008B/811